The Fibercraft Sampler

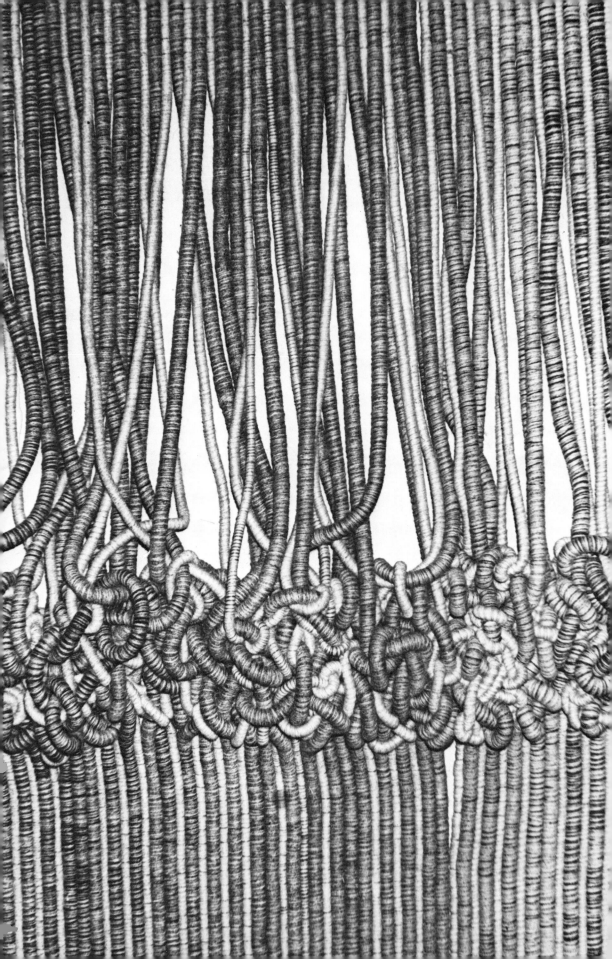

The Fibercraft Sampler

ELLEN APPEL

CHILTON BOOK COMPANY   RADNOR, PENNSYLVANIA

Copyright © 1978 by Ellen Appel   All Rights Reserved
Published in Radnor, PA, by Chilton Book Company and
simultaneously in Don Mills, Ontario, Canada,
by Thomas Nelson & Sons, Ltd.

Designed by Jean Callan King / Visuality

Manufactured in the United States of America

Library of Congress Cataloging in Publication Data
Appel, Ellen.
    The fibercraft sampler.

    (Chilton's creative crafts series)
    1. Textile crafts.   2. Fiberwork.
I. Title.
TT699.A66   746   78-7144
ISBN 0-8019-6643-4
ISBN 0-8019-6644-2 pbk.

All photographs and projects by the author unless
otherwise credited.
Illustrations by Priscilla Buttson Peterson.
Front cover, clockwise from upper right:
Hoop Tapestry by Rozann Johnson; coiled basket
by Janet Ennis; African basket by Mary Ann York;
Chicken basket by Janet Ennis; coiled basket by
Ellen Appel; needlelace circle by Ellen Appel.
In foreground: Ojo de Dios by Ellen Appel.
Back cover: Wrapped mirror by Robin Brisco;
Huichol yarnpainting, Anonymous.

1 2 3 4 5 6 7 8 9 0   7 6 5 4 3 2 1 0 9 8

To Janis and Janet
on the east and west coasts

Contents

Acknowledgments

Writing this book has been an exciting experience for me. In the course of my research, I had the opportunity to talk with so many fine artists who have chosen fiber as their medium. I especially enjoyed meeting Tom Fender, Kris Dey, Libby Platus and Debbe Moss, and I thank them all for taking the time to discuss their work with me.

My thanks also go to Rob Pulleyn, editor of *Fiberarts* magazine for sharing his views about the magazine, the medium and the state of the fiberarts. In addition, I'd like to extend my appreciation to Ann Robbins of the L.A. County Craft and Folk Art Museum, who put me in touch with many of the artists whose works appear in this book. Thanks also go to Suzie Walters of *Working Craftsman* magazine for providing me with names of some of my now-favorite fiber artists.

Marian Sanders, owner of the Rusty Needle fiber shop in Laguna Beach, California, deserves a special thank you. Marian was kind enough to help me locate local fiber artists and allow me to photograph their works day after day in her shop.

My appreciation also goes to the Los Angeles Bonaventure Hotel for providing me with a guided tour through the labyrinth of meeting rooms, ball rooms and restaurants where spectacular fiberworks hang. I acknowledge the assistance of the hotel and my guide from Paul C. Lasley & Associates.

My very special thanks go to Lydia M. Driscoll, crafts editor of Chilton Book Company. Lydia made each process run so smoothly, and only her special attention made it possible for this book to be published on schedule.

Most of all, I'd like to thank Janet Ennis, friend and fiber artist, who generously donated her services as critic, contributor and technical advisor from the day the book began to the day the manuscript was mailed.

The
Fibercraft
Sampler

WELCOME TO THE WORLD OF FIBERS

1–1 (*Opposite page*) Hoop tapestry. Rozann Johnson. 8′ x 5′. Wool, sisal and synthetic fibers woven in circular form. Appliqued with stuffed leather skins. Green and gold.

As the title suggests, this book is a sampler. Instead of an in-depth look at any one fibercraft, here's the entire spectrum of fibercrafts. This book presents coiling, wrapping, braiding, Mexican yarnpainting and ojos, knotting and weaving—all of today's most popular techniques. Every chapter includes basic instructions plus examples by some of this country's finest fiber artists. In *The Fibercraft Sampler,* "the medium is the message." Fibers are the most important ingredient. The ways to enjoy them, as you'll see, are unlimited.

THE STATE OF THE ART

Today, we appreciate fiberworks as much as the traditional fine arts. We find fiber constructions in galleries and homes. More and more people find that fiberworks add warmth and beauty to a home. Modern architects are also sensitive to the fibercrafts. They are increasingly choosing fiberworks in addition to, and sometimes instead of, paintings and sculptures for building interiors. New hotels, like the Los Angeles Bonaventure and many of the Hyatts, are filled with fiber pieces. Fibers seem to belong in the new buildings. The soft, textural and tactile qualities of the fibers go a long way to soften the straight lines of jet-age, steel and glass structures.

Today, fiber is a medium of expression for artists and craftspeople alike. *Fiberarts* magazine, the first publication devoted to all phases of fiber expression, used to be called the *Fibercraft Newsletter.* In a telephone interview, Rob Pulleyn, the magazine's editor, told a story to illustrate the medium's identity crisis. He talked about a two-story gallery that traditionally displayed all crafts, including fibers, on the second floor. Fine arts, on the other hand, appeared on the first floor. Today that same gallery shows fibers on the first floor.

Some call fiberworks *art;* others use the word *craft.* Personally I do not know which label is best. In truth, when the controversy is settled, the result will be the same: Fiber*crafts* or fiber*arts* will be responsible for some of the most beautiful pieces of creative expression today.

THE MEDIUM IS THE MESSAGE

An increasing number of artists now choose fibers as their medium of expression. In another decade, many of these same artists might have worked in paint or clay instead. It is no wonder fibers are becoming more important as a creative medium. Fibers offer unlimited possibilities as flat, two-dimensional design and three-dimensional sculpture. In addition, the same construction may possess two and three-dimensional qualities.

In the course of writing this book, I asked many artists why they chose fibers as their medium. Some gave the reason as an emotional response to the warmth, colors and textures of the materials. A few artists called the fibers "sensuous." "It's the textural manipulation—the texture, touch and being able to work with your hands," according to *Fiberarts* editor Rob Pulleyn.

Besides the pleasing qualities of the fibers and the satisfying nature of the techniques, there is also an exciting, experimental feeling that permeates the fibercrafts. You may be surprised to see how today's fiber artists adapt age-old techniques to modern fiber expression. All the strict rules and restrictions that applied to the traditional fibercrafts are now superseded by a "let-yourself-go" attitude.

In this book, you'll find a number of techniques to experiment with. Try each fibercraft alone, or combine them together. Invent your own techniques. Explore the vast array of materials. Use the instructions to learn the basics, and study the examples for inspiration. Treat this book as a celebration of the fibercrafts. Sample everything that appeals to you. Approach the fibercrafts with a spirit of adventure. And enjoy yourself.

ABOUT FIBERS

2–1 Baskets overflow with handspun, unspun, plied and unplied yarns.
Baskets, left to right, contain animal wools and hair; silk fibers; vegetable
fibers including cotton, linen, jute and sisal; and varied synthetics.

If your local fiber shop, or craft store, is anything like my local
fiber shop, you were probably overwhelmed the first time you
walked in and saw the rolls, skeins, hanks, bundles and cones
of fibers that overflow from cubbyholes, baskets and barrels.
Frankly I'm still overwhelmed whenever I go fiber shopping and
have to choose something for a project. Since I can take for-
ever just to decide whether to have carob chips, trail mix or
fresh strawberries on my frozen yogurt, picking out fibers is
quite a process for me.

To help you choose your fibers, this chapter describes the
animal, vegetable and synthetic fibers that are available to you.
Some fibers are better suited to one fibercraft than another.
For this reason, it is important to know the general characteristics of each fiber category. To get a closer look at many different fibers, write to a mail order source for sample cards.
These cards can be your first school of fibers. You can learn by
examining the fibers on the cards, browsing through yarn
shops and talking to the fiber artists you encounter there. Take
a look at the supply sources listing at the back of the book. The
list includes mail order sources and shops throughout the
country. Today, there is a source for fibers within reach of everyone.

ANIMAL WOOL AND HAIR

Wools are wiry, soft, coarse or light as a feather. The variation
between wools is considerable, but not surprising. Think of all

the breeds of dogs you know, and how their coats differ. Samoyeds, for example, have plush, furry coats while poodles have tight curls. In the same way, wools differ from animal to animal. The characteristics of a particular wool depend upon the animal it comes from, the species of the animal, where it lives and even what it eats. In addition, the wool quality varies on the same animal. By way of illustration, the wool on an animal's side is much finer than on the extremities. The undercoat is exceptionally fine and soft.

In spite of all the differences, all wools share certain properties. Wools are elastic, resilient and moisture-retentive. Because of its elasticity, wool regains its shape after stretching.

2–2 Untitled. Candace Crockett. 5'6" x 10'. Weaving executed in wool yarns and wool roving, rayon, jute and linen. Different fibers in varying weights create an exceptionally rich surface texture. Photographed at the Los Angeles Bonaventure Hotel.

The resilience makes the wool bounce back after crushing. When moist, wool provides warmth without feeling wet. Because of these valuable qualities, wools are suitable for warm fabrics, knitted goods and carpets. Most wools come from sheep. Other animals, however, also provide us with wool.

The llama, alpaca and vicuna have especially soft and luxurious wools. All three animals are native to South America and yield some of the finest quality wools in the world. The fibers are fluffy when brushed, and are used for fashion fabrics and knitwear. Llama and alpaca wools are similar to mohair. The very finest, rarest and most expensive is vicuna. In pre-Columbian times, the Inca royalty dressed in vicuna robes—a testimony to the rich, luxurious nature of the fiber.

The camel, a relative of the South American animals, has a fine soft undercoat and coarse outer hair. The undercoat has remarkable insulating properties and resistance to wrinkles. As a result, camel hair has become popular in coat fabrics. Many fiber artists love the undercoat fibers for their incredible softness and lightness. The coarse outer hairs add texture to wool yarns.

Goat hair, like camel hair, is also popular among fiber artists. For one reason, it has the strength needed for warp yarns plus an interesting texture and shine. Goat hair is strong, resilient, lustrous and more wrinkle-resistant than most wools. The look and feel of the fiber depends upon the goat it comes from. The Angora goat gives us mohair—a curly raw fiber that spins into a thin, feathery fiber or loopy yarn. Cashmere, from the Tibetan goat, is glossy, soft and elegant. Cashmere holds its shape exceptionally well and is found in high-priced knitwear and luxury fabrics. Laurel Scheeler, proprietor of "The Sheepish Grin" in New Jersey, says in her wonderfully descriptive catalog, "I keep a piece in my pocket to enjoy like a worry stone."

Other animals, in addition to those mentioned above, also provide raw fibers for fabrics, knitted goods and the fibercrafts. They range in texture from the Angora rabbit, with furry, ultrasoft fibers to horsehair (remember those stiff petticoats?). In addition, there is yet another animal fiber that is very unlike the

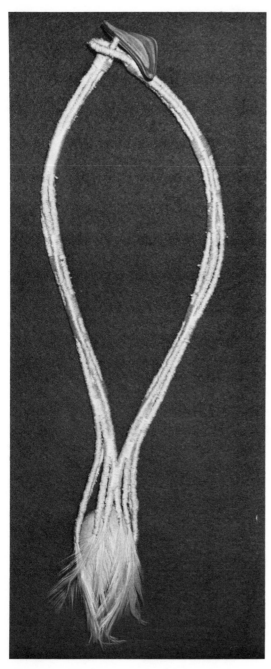

2–3 Silk necklace. Robin Brisco.
Hemp wrapped in raw silk. All white,
with driftwood clasp and feather
pendant.

others. That fiber is silk. Even the animal, the silkworm, doesn't look much like any other fiber-producing animal.

SILK

For thousands of years, silk production, called sericulture, was China's closely guarded secret. It was only through treachery and intrigue that sericulture ever spread beyond China's borders. The penalty for divulging the secret was death. In spite of this threat, the silkworms, and the mulberry trees they feed on, were smuggled from China centuries ago. Silk is now produced in the United States, Japan, Italy and other countries.

Silk is fine, lustrous, smooth and luxurious. It is no wonder the world beyond China's borders wanted to learn the secrets of silk production. Silk is the most elegant of fibers. When woven into cloth, it shimmers as it absorbs and reflects light and rustles as it moves. Silk is the traditional fiber in fine Oriental carpets and high quality garments. Silk may appear in the fibercrafts in the form of raw silk, thread or processed fabric.

VEGETABLE FIBERS

Vegetable fibers come from plants. They originate in the seed, leaf or stem of the plant. Of all the vegetable fibers, we are most familiar with cotton, one of the seed fibers. When the seed bursts open, a puff of white appears. That puff is the raw fiber that is picked and processed. Cotton is smooth, porous and moisture-absorbent. Often the characteristics of cotton vary, depending upon where the fiber is grown. Some cottons, like those grown in Egypt, are almost silk-like. Mercerized cotton is a processed variety familiar to most fiber artists. The process adds sheen, strength, colorfastness and receptivity to dyes.

Linen fibers, unlike cotton, are found in the stem of the flax plant. Linen is the most paradoxical of fibers. The processing is highly complicated; the fiber is difficult to dye, spin or weave; and the finished product is nonelastic and easily creased. On the other hand, linen is fine, strong, lustrous and highly absorbent. Linen has a long history of popularity in textiles. Despite all its disadvantages, its use dates back to ancient Egypt. In the fibercrafts, linen is a popular warp yarn and basketry core. Over the years, linen has been woven into towels, sheets and tablecloths. The term "linen closet" gives you an idea of the fiber's traditional purposes. It is ironic, however, that despite its name, our linen closets have been filled with cottons and polyesters for decades.

Hemp, also a stem fiber, is coarser than the cottons and linens and never enjoyed any popularity as a textile. In fact, hemp garments were once a sign of abject poverty. Hemp is valued nonetheless for its resistance to salt water decay. For this reason, hemp is found in twine, ropes, cables and sailcloth. Jute is yet another stem fiber. It is also coarse, but weaker than hemp or linen. Jute is used for ropes and rough fabric like burlap. It is a traditional favorite in knotting. Unfortunately jute decays more quickly than many other fibers. Therefore if you want your handiwork to be of museum quality and to last a hundred years, avoid this fiber.

Sisal, together with jute, were once the stars of the knotter's art. Sisal is stiff, strong and fairly inflexible. These qualities make sisal ideal for knotting and other three-dimensional techniques. Sisal also has an attractive sheen, and more longevity than jute.

There are many other plant fibers as well. Manila hemp, for example, is similar to hemp. Ramie, another plant fiber, is like linen. In addition, there is coir from coconuts, pina from pineapples and jusi from banana plants. It is certainly a sign of human ingenuity that our ancestors figured out how to create textiles from this incredible assortment of leaves, stems and seeds.

Vegetable fibers and animal fibers comprise the natural materials. Fibers in both these categories come from living, growing things. Except for asbestos, which is a mineral fiber, all others are synthetic.

2–4 The Announce. Susan B. Smith. 12′ long. Seven bells on jute, tarred sisal and recycled boat rope. Hangs on a stairwell to announce the arrival of visitors. Wrapped and knotted. Natural tones and hand-dyed, sun-bleached dusty red. Photograph courtesy of the author.

SYNTHETICS

I have a friend who thinks there are Acrilans inhabiting our forests. Those in the know (and that probably includes everyone but my friend) are aware that Acrilan is not a relative of the alpaca, but a brand name for a synthetic acrylic fiber. Unlike the natural fibers, synthetics result from chemical processing. There are two categories of synthetics: the regenerated fibers and the man-made fibers.

Rayon is a regenerated fiber. Originally, however, rayon was known as artificial silk although it didn't look very much like the natural fiber. Today we call rayon "rayon." We accept the synthetic fibers for what they are. Rayon is made from a natural base of cellulose and is then processed chemically. Rayons range from fine, shiny threads to coarse carpet yarns.

Man-made fibers, unlike the rayons, are made from chemicals alone. They are known as nylon, polyester, acrylic and polypropylene. Man-made fibers are used in knitwear, stockings and many categories of woven cloth from gabardine to chiffon. Man-made fibers are light, crease-resistant and nonabsorbent. As a result, they dry quickly and need little or no ironing. These properties more than partly account for their welcome in the modern world. For the fiber artist, synthetics increase the range of available materials. Many examples in this book show synthetics worked alone or combined with other fibers (Fig. 2–5).

TYPES OF YARN

Synthetic fibers are born as yarns. Natural fibers, unlike their man-made counterparts, go through several stages before the raw fiber turns to spun yarn. Raw fiber, processed yarn and all stages in between have a place in the fibercrafts. Stages include "carding" which straightens the fibers and "spinning" which turns them into long lengths.

Different types of yarns evolve as the raw fiber is processed. *Roving,* or *tops,* for example, consists of the long, parallel

2–5 Mechanistic Movement. Joan Michaels-Paque. 72″ x 40″ x 6″. Hitching and wrapping technique using synthetic fibers. In the collection of Alan and Barbara Schrinsky, Milwaukee. Photographed by Henry P. Paque.

15 ABOUT FIBERS

fibers that result from the carding process. Roving is a favorite for weft yarns in large weaving projects. It is fat, fluffy, cloud-soft and wonderful to touch.

Carded fibers are spun into yarns. Handspun yarns, as the name suggests, are spun by hand, usually on a spinning wheel. Handspuns are characteristically uneven and highly textured. Some handspuns are more regular than others, depending upon the skills and objectives of the spinner. Machine-spun yarns, unless they are meant to look like handspuns, are regular and even.

After spinning, by machine or by hand, the yarn is a long, continuous strand. A single strand of spun fiber is called a one-ply yarn. When two strands are twisted together, the result is a two-ply yarn. Multiple-ply yarns are also available.

Yarns are available in many other forms. Variegated yarns, for example, combine strands of different color or texture. Tweed yarns have tiny nubs in contrasting colors. Chenilles are velvet-like. These are just a few types of yarns. There are many, many more—enough to fill another book.

CHOOSING YOUR FIBERS

You have a wide selection when it comes to choosing fibers for a piece. Some decisions are, of necessity, based on the requirements of each fibercraft. For example, braiding fibers should have little or no stretch. Consequently, cotton or linen would be better to work with than bouncy wools. This book presents general guidelines chapter by chapter to help you select your fibers according to the needs of your project. Before you begin any project, therefore, take a look at the materials section in each chapter.

Other considerations, like color and texture, are based on personal taste alone. Some artists work in several textures of the same color. Others choose different colors in similar textures. When in doubt, hold the yarns together before you purchase them. If the combination looks right to you, try it.

Price is also something to think about. Truthfully, fine fibers

2–6 Fiber pocket. Nan Hackett Joe. Woven in handspun wools and samoyed hair.

2–7 Detail of KCET TV set. Debbe Moss. Processed cloth acts as warp and weft fibers. See Figure 7–3 for a larger section. Photograph courtesy of the artist.

are expensive. For any project, try to judge in advance exactly how many ounces, pounds or even hundreds of pounds of fiber you will need. Then determine which yarns are within your price range. It is easy to run out of fiber before you finish a project. Every artist does from time to time. I've done it more than once, and ended up doubling my anticipated yarn costs. When you select your yarns, ask for help from salespeople. If they have been selling fibers long enough, they will probably be able to guide you.

Also consider durability in choosing fibers. If the piece is to be hung, various environmental conditions will affect its longevity. Certain fibers, like jute, do not belong outdoors. In contrast, many synthetics hold up remarkably well in adverse weather conditions. In addition, avoid bright colors if you plan to hang your work in a sunny area. Most dyes fade in strong sunlight, and you might be disappointed when your fiber piece loses its brilliance.

No matter where you live, many fibers are within reach. If there isn't a local fiber shop in your area, try your neighborhood craft store or one of the many mail order companies who offer absolutely beautiful products on a national basis. Stanley Berroco, for example, has a fabulous fibercraft line. Names range from "Bim Bam" to "Zoom Zoom," and fibers range from plush and elegant to nubby and rough spun. Lily Mills also has a comprehensive fiber line with a wide selection of handweaving yarns. If you can't find these products at your local knitting shop, variety or craft store, why not suggest that they stock them.

As you sample the fibercrafts, also sample as many fibers as you can. Don't be afraid to try anything. If you own a samoyed or collie, save the hairs whenever you brush the dog's coat. Some cat hairs are also usable, as long as you aren't making a gift for someone who's allergic to cats. Dog hair, cat hair and even human hair have a place in the fibercrafts. Also don't forget about processed cloth, leather and paper. If you think about it, you can probably add to this list of unique fibers.

When you next visit your yarn shop or send for a mail order catalog, you'll no doubt see all the fibers mentioned in this chapter. The wide variety of yarns may still seem overwhelming. Now however, you'll have a better idea of how to choose between them.

COILING: BASKETMAKING & BEYOND

3–1 (*Opposite page*) Circular convex wall hanging. Joan Michaels-Paque. 36″ diameter. Red and black Lily Mills soft sheen fiber worked into figure 8 coiling. Stuffed. Commissioned by Lily Mills, Shelby, NC. Photograph by Henry P. Paque.

Once, I took a trip to the Philippines. It was quite an adventure for me, and I made the most of it by traveling to the most exotic places in the country, from Banaue to Zamboanga. One day while I was traveling, it began to rain. Since my visit to the Philippines was during the typhoon season, this was hardly unusual. However, this time the rain struck while I was in the mountains far from the city. In these remote mountain areas, life is still primitive. Homes are grass-roofed huts, and electricity is scarce. While I watched the rain, a man passed by with a basket covering his head and shoulders. I asked what he was wearing and the answer was a "raincoat." At first, I thought the reply was a poor translation to English. On looking again, however, I realized that the basket (although a far cry from a London Fog with epaulets) was indeed protection from the rain. It was designed for that purpose long ago, and works quite well today.

To this day, villagers in the Philippines prepare rice in rice baskets, store potatoes in potato baskets and keep fruit in fruit baskets (Fig. 3–2). Like the rattan "raincoat," each basket is tailored to a specific need. Shapes are rooted in tradition.

3–2 Philippino children preparing rice in a flat basket.

Often by looking at a basket, you can know what is inside. Certain shapes hold particular foods. Others have work functions. Still more are reserved for ceremonial occasions.

To tourists and fiber artists, baskets are objects of beauty. We buy them and make them to put on display, fill with seashells or grow plants in. But in primitive pockets of the Philippines and other countries, baskets are still necessary for catching fish, preparing food, presenting wedding gifts and protecting yourself from the rain.

Basketmaking was born thousands of years ago to fill fundamental needs. Whether it was carrying food or babies, there was a basket for every purpose. Even today, in cultures throughout the world, baskets are as common as pots, pans and other manufactured items are to us. In fact, whether the technique is coiling, twining or weaving, people still make and use baskets as they have for centuries.

Our baskets, on the other hand, can be anything we want them to be. Although they can, and often do, have practical functions, the emphasis in contemporary basketry is on the container's appearance. It is primarily a sculptural form. If it holds something as well, that is the choice of the basketmaker.

In modern basketry, shape and materials depend only on preference. There's no need to worry about whether or not the materials are waterproof or traditional. By the same token, designs may incorporate open spaces, and shapes no longer must be prescribed by custom. Today's basketmaker is completely free to experiment and explore.

Coiling is a basic technique for basketmakers. Among American Indian cultures, coiling techniques are used in Hopi, Navajo and Pima baskets to name just a few. There are coiled baskets to be found in the Americas, Asia, Africa and from history's early beginnings. This chapter explores coiling in contemporary basketry and sculpture.

THE COILING PROCESS

Two words come up often in coiling: the *core* and the *weft.* Basically, in coiling, a *core* is wrapped with a more flexible

3-3 Coiled basket. Ginger Luters. Strips of print fabric wrapped on sisal; coils stitched in perle cotton. Photograph courtesy of the artist.

fiber called the *weft.* As the core is wrapped, it is shaped into coils. At the same time, coils are stitched together and built into sculptural forms.

Coiling is often thought of as a basketry technique. However, it is not only a basketry technique, nor is it *the only* basketry technique. If this chapter seems to be the "basketmaking chapter," it is because coiling is so well-suited to contemporary basketry (Fig. 3-3).

Making a basket is a good way to learn coiling. Instructions in this chapter show how to make a basic rounded shape. After learning the techniques, it is easy to understand why coiling is so popular among today's basketmakers.

Coiling is also a perfect way to build up three-dimensional forms of any kind. This includes free-standing sculptures, wall hangings and ornaments as well as baskets. Coiling also adds interest when combined with other fiber techniques. Coiling is versatile. It lends itself to interesting shaping possibilities and an enormous variety of materials.

25 COILING

MATERIALS

The core and weft are the basic coiling materials. Aside from these essentials, little else is required. The only other tools are scissors and a blunt yarn needle with a hole that is large enough for the weft.

For the core, choose a material that is sturdy yet flexible. Jute, sisal, linen, cotton piping, clothesline and seagrass are all easy to find and appropriate as cores (Fig. 3–4). In addition, the Lily Mills line now includes a special basket core. Their new core is lightweight and available in different thicknesses.

Thickness is an important consideration in choosing a core. Scale the core to the size of the basket. Small baskets are more attractive with thinner cores. For very large baskets, thick upholstery piping is particularly good. As a rule, the thicker the core, the faster the work progresses.

There are other considerations as well. With roving, for example, a basket will be softer than with jute. One fiber artist, Janet Ennis, prefers seagrass to other cores because of its fragrance. "The pleasant aroma of the seagrass remains even after the basket is completed," the artist explains.

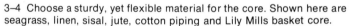

3–4 Choose a sturdy, yet flexible material for the core. Shown here are seagrass, linen, sisal, jute, cotton piping and Lily Mills basket core.

The choice of weft, or wrapping materials, is almost endless. You can use anything from handspun wools to processed cloth. Your weft simply must be flexible enough to wrap around the core. For the biggest selection, your best bet is a special fiber shop. If there's one nearby, plan to spend some time looking around. Since so many fibers are wonderful for the weft, you'll probably want to check out every corner of the store.

Experiment with whatever textures and colors appeal to you. Handspun wool, goat hair, camel hair and linen are popular basketry fibers. For shine, many beautiful gold threads, silks and shimmering rayons are often available. For special textures, try fluffy brushed wools, loopy mohairs or nubby boucles.

The only yarns that don't seem to work well are soft knitting yarns or fibers with too much stretch. However, there are exceptions in these categories as well. If in doubt, why not experiment with a small sample.

For the basket demonstrated here, materials are Stanley Berroco's Nubs 'n Slubs, and Homespun Nature Wool, unplied handspun wool and Lily Mills basket core.

MAKING A BASKET

Figure 3–5 shows the nearly completed basket and Figure 3–6a to e shows how to get started to make a coiled basket. It is important to note how materials are held in the photographs. If you are right-handed, follow the photos and illustrations exactly. In other words, hold the coils in your left hand, and the wrapping materials in your right hand. If you are left-handed, work the opposite way. It is essential to hold your materials correctly. Otherwise, working will seem awkward and yarns will tangle.

It is also important to keep the working side facing you. For most baskets, this is the outside. For low, shallow bowls however, it is preferable to work on the inside. When deciding

3–5 The nearly completed basket which uses the lazy squaw stitch, the figure 8 stitch and imbrication.

which way to work, determine which side will show most in the finished basket. Keep that side facing you.

Starting the Base

To begin, cut 3 to 4 feet of yarn. Taper the end of the basket core with scissors. Lay the yarn end against the core. Wind the loose yarn toward the tapered end of the core. Keep winding until you are about ½″ from the end (Fig. 3–6a).

Be sure to hold your materials as shown in Figure 3–6a. If you are right-handed, point the tapered end toward the right, and wind the yarn toward you from over the top. I find this is

3–6a Starting the base near tapered end of core.

3–6b Folding tapered end in and winding around folded core.

the best way to work although many basketmakers prefer winding from the front to the back. Experiment and see which way is most comfortable for you.

To make the first coil, fold in the wrapped end of the core. Wind the yarn around both pieces of the core. The result is a loop that is wrapped with yarn (Fig. 3–6b).

3–6c Forming the first coil.

3–6d Forming coils by winding around core and stitching the new coil to the one below it. When you have less than 2″ of weft, add on a new length (fig. 3–17).

3–6e Adding new weft, or core, by tapering both ends and wrapping together.

Forming a Coil

Next, bend the loop around to form a circular coil. Stitch through the loop (Fig. 3–6c).

Continue winding yarn around the core and forming coils as you wrap. After every few winds, stitch the new coil to the one below it (Fig. 3–6d). Choose between the "figure 8," "lazy squaw" and "lace" stitches (Figs. 3–8, 3–9, 3–10). Lazy squaw stitches are used in the base for this basket.

Adding New Weft

When you have less than 2″ of weft, cut another 3 to 4 foot length, and lay the new yarn against the core (Fig. 3–6d). Wrap over the new end a few times with the original weft yarn. Then holding the original yarn against the core, wrap the core with the new yarn.

Splicing Core

If you run out of core, untwist the ends of the old and new core; taper the ends with scissors; and twist ends together (Fig. 3–6e). To make the process as easy as possible, be sure to splice the core where there's enough weft to wrap and stitch over the splice.

COILING STITCHES

In the coiling process, coils are joined to one another with stitches. The choice of stitch determines the strength and design of the basket coiling. Of the stitches shown, the figure 8 is the firmest and least visible stitch. That is why it is a particular favorite of basketmakers. The lazy squaw stitch and lace stitch are also popular. Each of these three stitches is described and illustrated step-by-step. In all the examples, there are two coils involved in the stitching process. Here, the coil being wrapped is referred to as the *top* or *upper* coil. The one already wrapped is the *lower* coil.

3–7 Coiled basket. Sharon La Pierre. 20″ high. Lazy squaw stitches emphasize color changes in the basket's design. Coiled wool on a gourd base. Photograph courtesy of the artist.

Figure 8 Stitch

The figure 8 stitch makes an especially stable basket. In addition, if the same yarn is used throughout the basket, the stitching barely shows at all. Most coiling examples in this chapter are done with figure 8 stitching.

Figure 3–8 shows how to do this stitch. Hold the yarn behind the top coil (Fig. 3–8a). Stitch over the top coil, behind the

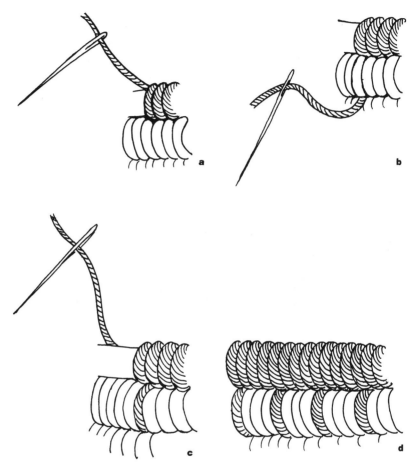

3–8 The figure 8 stitch.

lower coil and through to the front (Fig. 3–8b). Next, stitch over the lower coil and behind the top coil (Fig. 3–8c). Wind the yarn around the top coil a few times between each figure 8 stitch (Fig. 3–8d).

Lazy Squaw Stitch

Despite the name, the lazy squaw stitch hardly takes less time or effort than the other stitches. In fact, since the stitch is so visible, it takes more thought. Neatness counts more than usual and you must keep track of spacing between stitches.

The advantage of the lazy squaw stitch is the pattern created in the basket. Take a look at Sharon La Pierre's basket in Figure 3–7. In this basket, color changes are dramatized with these stitches.

Here's how to do this stitch (Fig. 3–9). Hold the yarn behind the top coil (Fig. 3–9a). Stitch over both the upper and lower coils, and bring the yarn back up behind the upper coil (Fig. 3–9b). Wind it around the top coil a few times between lazy squaw stitches (Fig. 3–9c).

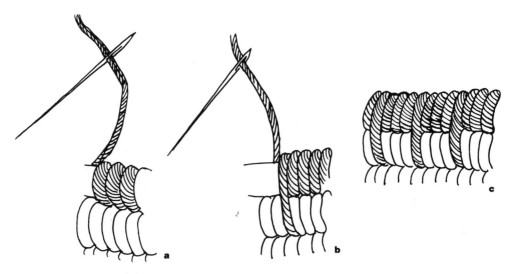

3–9 The lazy squaw stitch.

Lace or Mariposa Stitch

The lace stitch creates a knotted pattern between coils. With heavy yarns, a pattern of open spaces results. If wider spaces are desired, wrap the yarn around the stitch 2 or 3 times (Fig. 3–10c). A particularly interesting way to use the lace stitch is in conjunction with beads. You can see how well they work together in Marian Sander's basket in Figure 3–11.

Here's how to do this stitch (Fig. 3–10). Hold the yarn behind the upper coil (Fig. 3–10a). Stitch over the upper and lower

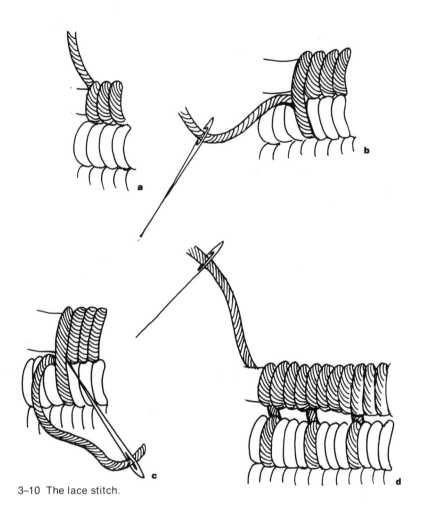

3–10 The lace stitch.

coils and come up behind the lower coil. Keep the yarn to the left of the stitch (Fig. 3–10b). Bring the needle horizontally across the stitch (Fig. 3–10c). Bring the yarn back up behind the top coil. Wind the yarn around the top coil a few times between each lace stitch (Fig. 3–10d).

SHAPING COILS

When it comes to shaping a basket, there are many approaches to take. The basket shown here in process has a clas-

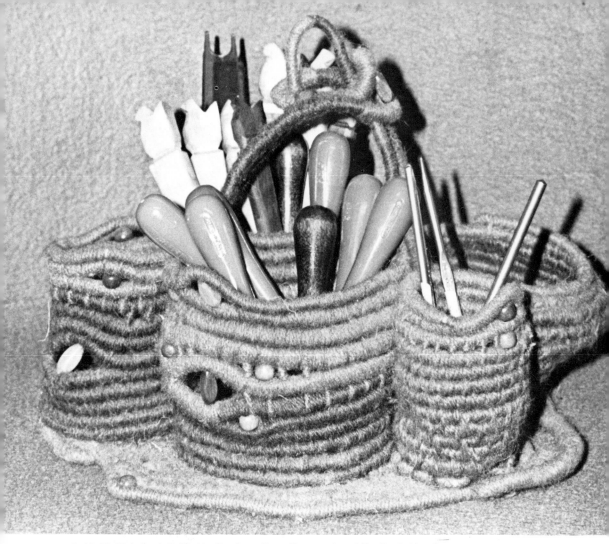

3–11 Multiple basket. Marian Sanders. From the counter at the Rusty Needle fiber shop in Laguna Beach, California. This multiple basket usually overflows with crochet needles, weaving picks, rug hooks and other implements. Note the lace stitches and beads between coils.

sic shape. It tapers outward and inward for a typical rounded shape. However, baskets may also be cone-shaped, tapered to a narrow opening or free-form. Sharon La Pierre's frog basket in Figure 3–12 is especially interesting. The shape itself is simple, but the outcome is a wide-mouthed frog. With practice, it is possible to build coils into representational forms. It is also possible to twist and turn coils into abstract, irregular shapes. It is also possible to fold coils back on themselves instead of continuing the circular motion. This technique is helpful in creating openings and building noncontainer shapes. Whatever shape you choose, be sure to keep stitches and coils tight. Often a gentle pull on the core helps to tighten a coil. In fact, it's not even necessary to make baskets at all. When you learn

3–12 Frog basket. Sharon La Pierre. 18″ high. A wide-mouthed basket with a whimsical approach. Figure 8 coiling. Crocheted details. Wool. Photograph courtesy of the artist.

37 COILING

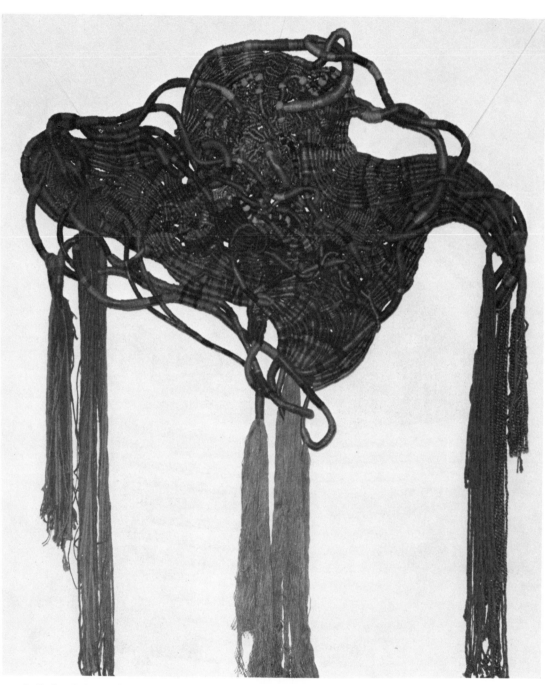

3–13 Quetzalcoatl. B. J. Adams. 89″ x 76″ x 7″. Coiled, knotted and wrapped sculpture is sisal, jute, Maxi-cord, cotton, linen, wool and synthetics. Three curved plastic rods provide support. Reds, purples and earth tones. Photograph courtesy of the artist.

coiling, it is easy to see how well-suited this method is to three-dimensional designs of all kinds (Fig. 3–13).

Shaping the Basket

To form the sides of the basket, stitch the new coil on top rather than around the previous coil. To make the shape wider, place the new coil on the outer edge of the coil below. To narrow a shape, place the new coil on the inner edge of the coil below. For steep sides, line up the new coils with the previous coils. Figure 3–14 shows the basket in process.

Build up the basket sides, working in patterns, pictures and designs as you wrap. The coils in process (Fig. 3–15) are decorated with *imbrication* (Fig. 3–21). The yarn change was accomplished with blind stitches (Fig. 3–20).

DECORATING COILS

Most designs are worked into the coils as you wrap. This requires advance planning and an ability to think from the bot-

3–14 This basket tapers slightly outward and then inward for a typical shape. The sides are done in figure 8 stitches; the base is lazy squaw stitches.

3–15 Imbrication and color change adds interesting texture and design.

3–16 Coiled basket. Sharon La Pierre. 20″ high. Colors create a vertical pattern. Figure 8 coiling in wool. Gourd base. Photograph courtesy of the artist.

tom up. Create designs by wrapping the coils with yarns in different textures and colors. Using the techniques illustrated, it is easy to change yarns as frequently as you wish. Figure 3–16 is an excellent example of color design.

Changing Colors

Lay the new color against the core (Fig. 3–17a). Wrap over the new end a few times with the original yarn (Fig. 3–17b). Holding the original yarn against the core, wrap the core with the new color (Fig. 3–17c).

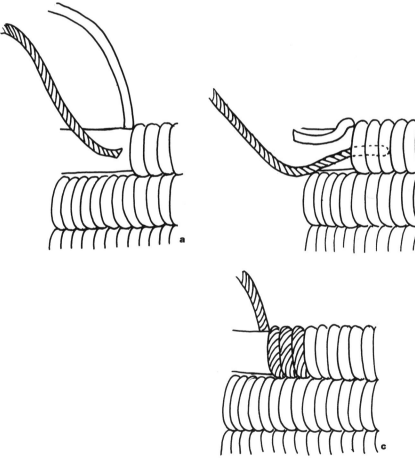

3–17 Changing colors of yarn or adding weft.

Use this method when you change colors completely. If you are going to alternate colors, it is easier to carry along the original color as described below.

Carrying Along Yarns

Carry two or more yarns along with the core. Wrap with one yarn and hold the other(s) against the core (Fig. 3–18). As you wrap the core, be sure to hide all the other yarns completely. To change colors, just switch yarns. In other words, hold the wrapping yarn against the core and wrap with one of the other yarns.

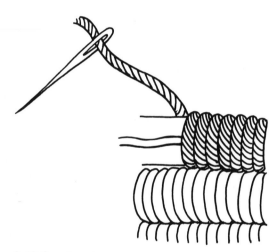

3–18 Carrying along yarn.

It is a good idea to carry yarns along if you plan to alternate colors. Carrying along two or three yarns is fairly easy. More than that, however, is cumbersome.

Multiple Wrapping

Thread two or more yarns through the needle; wrap them around the core simultaneously (Fig. 3–19). This technique is

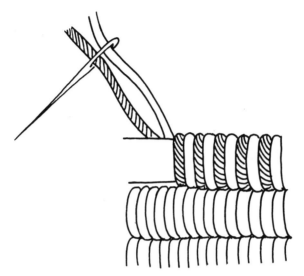

3-19 Multiple wrapping.

especially good with closely related colors or textures. Multiple wrapping is also a time saver. When yarns are really thin, wrapping a few inches can seem like an eternity. Rather than avoiding thin yarns, it is a good idea to wrap with more than one. With three yarns for example, even the skinniest yarns don't make coiling feel like an endless process. Nubby, brushed and looped yarns seem to blend into one another and are highly recommended for multiple wrapping.

STITCHING PATTERNS

You'll notice, when you change colors, that even figure 8 stitches are obvious. No matter which of the standard stitches you choose, a pattern develops whether you want it or not. Although stitching patterns are often very beautiful, there are times you'd rather avoid them. Use a blind stitch at these times instead of the more visible stitches.

43 COILING

Blind Stitch

On the inside of the basket, stitch through the yarn on the lower coil (Fig. 3–20). Wrap only once or twice between blind stitches. The blind stitch does not show outside the basket, but it is not as firm as the other stitches. Use it only when necessary for the pattern development.

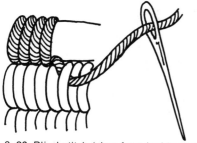

3–20 Blind stitch (view from inside basket).

Imbrication

Imbrication, with the same or contrasting yarn, creates textural interest (Fig. 3–21). The technique leaves a loopy effect on the outside of the basket. Sometimes, the term "klikitat" is used interchangeably with imbrication. The word refers to the Klikitat of the Pacific Northwest, a group known for their imbricated baskets.

The method described here is similar to the classic klikitat. Besides yarns, some interesting fibers for imbrication are ribbon, raffia, leather cords and felt strips.

3–22 Imbrication is a method used to create textural interest.

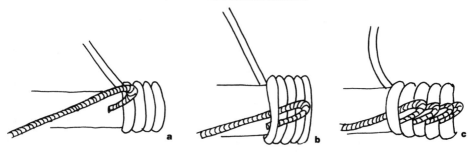

3-21 Silver Elegance. Mary Ann York. 6" x 7". Mohair, looped yarns and fleece are worked into this multitextured, imbricated basket. In neutral tones, including silver, gray and white. Photograph by Rich Tardif.

Create a loop with the new yarn (Fig. 3–22a). Wrap over the loop at least once (Fig. 3–22b). Repeat the process along the length of the core (Fig. 3–22c). After every few winds, stitch as usual. Make the loops as large or small as you like. It is not necessary to keep the loops absolutely uniform.

APPLIED MATERIALS

Feathers, beads, buttons, shells and leather scraps are easy and fun to add. Mary Ann York is one basketmaker who applies

3–23 (*Opposite page*) Conical hanging basket. Mary Ann York. 12″ x 10″. Ermine tails, shells and tin cones decorate this coiled basket. Earth tones in goat hair and camel hair. Photograph by Rich Tardif.

3–24 Coiled basket. Dea Hackett. Wools and novelty yarns. Feathers line the upper edge of this coiled basket.

materials freely. For example, take a look at her basket in Figure 3–23. As you can see, it's lavished with shells, ermine tails and tin cones.

Feathers

Feathers can be used to add grace, color and texture to a design (Fig. 3–24). To add feathers, strip excess fuzz from the end of the feather. Pointing the feather to the right, place the end against the core. Wind the wrapping yarn around both the feather and the core (Fig. 3–25).

Beads

Figures 3–11 and 3–12 are examples of how beads can be used to enhance your design. For a row of beads along a coil,

47 COILING

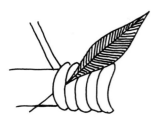

3–25 Inserting feathers into coils.

string beads (or buttons, shells and similar materials) on a separate piece of yarn. Cover at least 3″ with the wrapping yarn (Fig. 3–26a). Slide a bead up to the core; wind the wrapping cord on the other side of the bead (Fig. 3–26b).

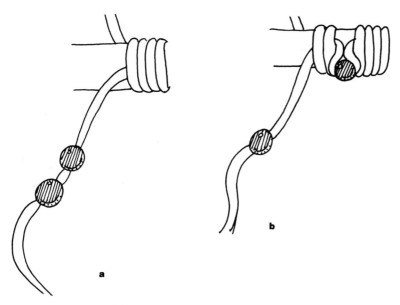

3–26 Stringing beads into coils.

Beads Between Coils

To use beads between coils, bring the needle over the top coil, through the bead, behind the lower coil and through to

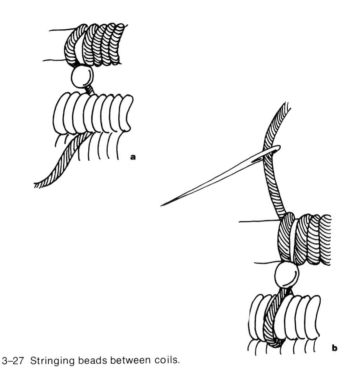

3-27 Stringing beads between coils.

the front (Fig. 3–27a). Bring the needle over the lower coil, back through the bead and behind the top coil (Fig. 3–27b).

ENDING COILED PROJECTS

The classic way to end a basket appears in Figure 3–28. When it comes to ending your coiling, this simple method is just one possibility. Every artist solves the problem differently. If you look back through this chapter, you'll see a range of ideas. If you choose the classic approach, refer back to Figures 3–5 and 3–28. If you prefer decorative endings, try feathers, shells, beads or other materials along the top edge (Fig. 3–24). As in shaping, decorating and stitching, it is exciting to experiment with endings (Fig. 3–29).

3–29 (*Opposite page*) Christmas ornaments. Ginger Luters. Wrapping and coiling in wool and shiny rayons. Tassel endings.

3–28 The classic way to end a basket.

Ending the Basket

When the basket reaches the desired height, taper the core with scissors (Fig. 3–5). Wind yarn around the core as before. When you reach the tapered end, stitch the yarn around the end and the coil below it. Stitch the yarn through the last few winds for a very regular finished edge (Fig. 3–28).

WRAPPING: ON ITS OWN

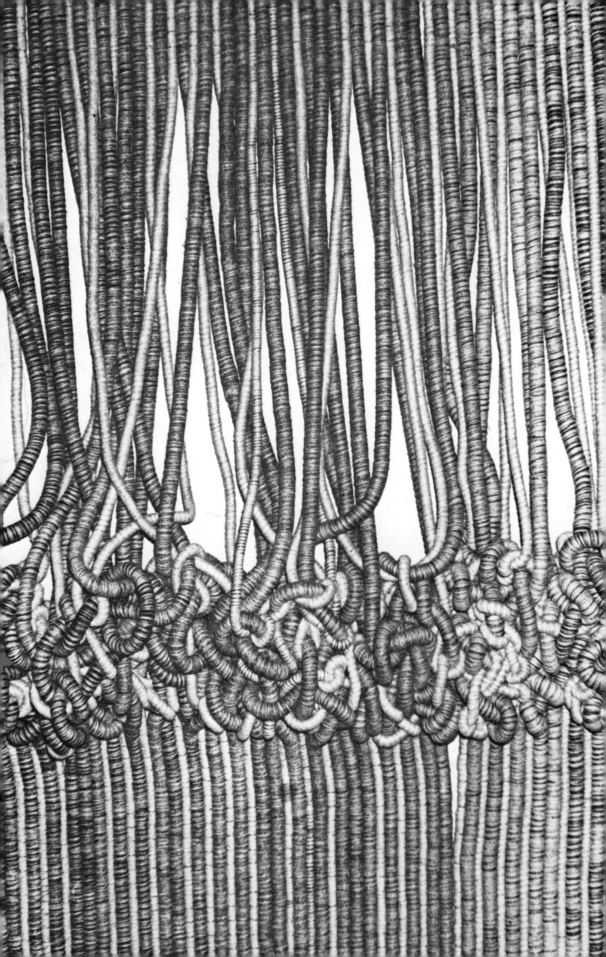

Until recently, wrapping was considered an adjunct to the other fiber techniques—helpful, but in the background of the fibercraft world. Most times, wrapping was simply a practical solution to problems like keeping ends together in a tassel. Now however, many fiber artists have discovered the artistic potential of wrapping, whether it is in combination with other fibercrafts or all alone. It all depends upon how you wrap, what you wrap with and what you do with the wrapped cords.

Today, wrapping appears over and over again in the fibercrafts. Sometimes a wrapped cord spills from a weaving. Other times a wrapped cord extends beyond the tightly coiled spirals in a basket. Wrapping is dramatic, and often the most striking element in a piece.

In this chapter, wrapping is the star. Wrapping appears either completely on its own, or as the featured technique in a piece. Of all the techniques in this book, wrapping is probably the most simple. Yet it is fascinating to see all its possibilities. The basic method never changes, but different approaches, color choices and materials account for radically different results.

Wrapped works come in all colors, shapes and sizes. In this chapter, you'll see wrapped works as small as 6" and large enough for a hotel ballroom (Fig. 4–1). Some stand in neat, geometric lines. Others have an organic feel. Colors and patterns are equally varied. The range stretches from subtle and monochromatic to vivid visual exercises.

Take a look through the examples in this chapter. Later browse through the other chapters and take note of all the wrapped elements that mix in with the other fibercrafts. Wrapping is exciting, no matter how you use it. After you experiment with the technique, you'll see what I mean.

THE WRAPPING PROCESS

Wrapping is as easy as it sounds. Like coiling, the wrapping process covers a core with a flexible fiber. Unlike coiling, however, the wrapped core is not stitched into coils. Instead, wrapped elements hang separately or join together in rows or free-form patterns.

4–2 Star Shroud. Susan Nelson. 6″ x 6″ x 3″. Memorializing the death of Elvis Presley. Headlined newspapers tied with goat hair wrapped cords. Interwoven with one gold Lurex wrapped cord.

This chapter explores basic wrapping and *no-core* wrapping. Basic wrapping is the simple, "wrap-a-fiber-around-a-core" method. Most often, the core is a single element, like thick sisal or a plastic tube (Fig. 4–3). Other times the core is a group of fibers, like several strands of jute or yarn.

In no-core wrapping, there's no special core at all. Instead, the core fibers and wrapping fibers are interchangeable. One benefit of no-core wrapping is having exposed sections, hanging tassels, beginnings and endings that match the wrappings. In addition, interchangeable fibers make it easy to alternate colors and create special effects.

4–3 Kris Dey at work. The artist wraps with a machine invented especially for the wrapping process. As the machine rotates the core material, in this case a PVC tube, the artist feeds fabric strips onto it.

The no-core technique, with its many benefits, is demonstrated in the sample belt project shown in Figure 4–15.

MATERIALS

For almost all wrapping projects, you'll need a core, the wrapping fiber, scissors and a yarn needle. The most common core materials are jute, sisal and cotton piping. All are sturdy, flexible and comparatively inexpensive. Use a single length of fiber for your core, or group several strands together. Almost anything is appropriate as core material. *Anything* can be fibers like those mentioned above, plastic tubes as in Kris Dey's work in Figure 4–3 or even ready-made baskets as in Barbara Chapman's Festival Ornament in Figure 4–11.

When it comes to the wrapping fibers, your choice is even greater. There's only one limit, and it's not much of a limitation. The sole requirement for the wrapping fibers is that they must have enough flexibility for winding around a core. Use any textures, from the smoothest, skinniest unplied yarns to the nubbiest textured boucles. Plied and unplied wool are popular in wrapping. Waxed linen, gold cords and shiny rayons are also popular, especially over thin cores. Some artists wrap with fabric strips. Print fabrics provide particularly interesting results.

If you plan to join wrapped elements, you'll also need nylon thread, waxed linen, unwaxed linen, goat hair or another strong fiber. Strength is the most important requirement for fibers that join wrapped elements. The heavier the wrapped element, the stronger your fiber will have to be.

For "no-core" projects, choose thin cords that blend well together. As the name suggests, no separate core fiber is needed. To make a belt like the one shown in Figure 4–15, choose an assortment of shiny synthetics in at least three different colors.

BASIC WRAPPING TECHNIQUES

Making a Center-Pull Ball
No matter what you're wrapping, whether it is a length of sisal or plastic tube, the process is much easier if you work with a center-pull ball of yarn. The ball is comfortable to hold; it releases yarn as needed; and there are no long ends to tangle. Make one center-pull ball of yarn from each wrapping fiber you will be using. Follow Figures 4–5a and 4–5b for making the center-pull ball.

Starting to Wrap
Figures 4–6a and 4–6b show the basic wrapping technique. If you are right-handed, hold the core in your left hand and the

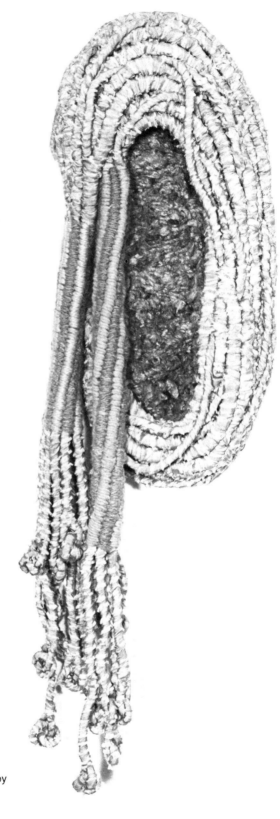

4–4 Silk. Lou Ridder. 30″ x 10″. Silk fabric
wrapped over jute. Techniques include
wrapping, coiling and twining. Yarns include
handspun silk, wool and linen. Photograph by
Jackie Sherman.

4–5a To make a center-pull ball, leaving 3″ of yarn hanging free, wrap yarn around fingers. Change directions as you wrap. Remove yarn from fingers when wrapping becomes cumbersome. Keep shaping the ball, while taking care not to cover the original end.

4–5b Put a rubber band around the ball of yarn. Tuck in the wrapping end. When using the ball, always pull yarn from the center.

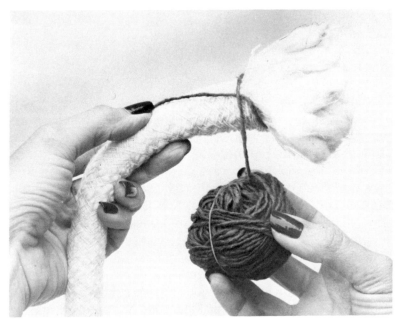

4–6a When starting to wrap, hold yarn end against core. Wind yarn around core, completely covering the yarn and core.

4–6b To cover the core, keep winding yarn onto the core. Change yarns or add new colors according to the illustrations which follow.

wrapping materials in your right hand. If you are left-handed, reverse the process.

COLOR AND PATTERN

Whether you prefer dramatic or subtle color changes, you'll probably wish to vary colors from time to time. Often the yarn itself provides color changes. For example, space-dyed yarns turn into thick stripes in the wrapping process.

Some of the most exuberant color patterns appear in Kris Dey's work. You can see the pattern movement in Bopus in the color section. According to artist Kris Dey, all her works explore "linear systems," which are translated into strips of striped cloth. Dey layers these strips, or linear systems, on plastic tubes. When tubes line up, they interact with one another in brilliant, almost pulsating patterns.

In contrast, Tom Fender's work shows subtle and gradual color changes. Take a look at Figure 4–1 for an exquisite example of his wrapped work. Fender's medium is wool, with sisal as the foundation. In this work, the movement of wrapped elements creates patterns. "The yarn is a three-dimensional line, and in wrapping that one line creates thousands of spirals," comments the artist. "When the element moves in any direction, the spiral bends." Later, Fender adds, "It would be fascinating to x-ray a piece and see what happens to all the spirals and lines."

The directions below demonstrate different methods of working with color. The method for starting new colors is the same as the method for adding new yarns. Add new yarns according to these directions each time your original wrapping yarn is used up.

Starting New Colors or New Yarns

To start a new color or yarn, lay the new yarn against the core (Fig. 4–7a). Wrap over the new end a few times with the original yarn (Fig. 4–7b). Hold the original end against the core. Wrap the core with the new yarn, covering the original yarn end (Fig. 4–7c).

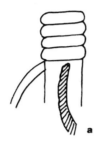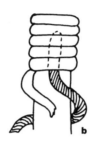

4–7 Starting new colors or new yarns.

Use this method to add new yarns when you run out of the original wrapping yarn. If you are going to alternate yarns, however, it is easier to carry along the original yarn as shown in Figure 4–8.

Alternating Yarns

To alternate yarns, keep two or more yarns parallel to the cord. Wrap with one yarn and hold the others against the core. As you wrap, hide the other yarns completely. To change colors, switch yarns. In other words, hold the wrapping yarn against the core, and wrap with one of the other yarns (Fig. 4–8).

4–8 Alternating yarns.

4-9 Multiple wrapping.

Multiple Wrapping

Figure 4-9 shows how to wrap several yarns around the core simultaneously. Unless you prefer a twisted effect, take care not to twist yarns as you wrap.

Short Wraps

To make a short section of wrappings follow Figure 4-10. To start, loop one end of the wrapping cord, and lay this loop over the core. Wrap the cord around the loop and the core at the same time. As you near the looped end, thread the wrapping cord through the loop (Fig. 4-10a). Pull the other end of the wrapping cord. This will pull the loop under and secure the end (Fig. 4-10b). Trim ends. This technique is convenient whenever you are wrapping small areas. For example, you may desire

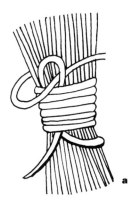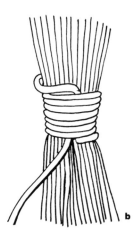

4–10 Short wraps.

short wrapped areas that alternate with exposed sections of core. Or else, you may wish to add another yarn after the core is already wrapped.

VARIATIONS AND ENDINGS

Take a look at the wrapping examples in this chapter to get ideas for how to use the wrapped elements. As you'll see, some artists weave the elements together with visible or invisible yarns. Others wrap the elements around one another and add on bells or tassels (Fig. 4–11). To keep elements where you want them, stitch them at every juncture with matching yarn or invisible thread.

If your core is several strands of yarn, try "split wrapping" or "figure 8 wrapping." Both techniques are interesting variations on the basic wrap and are shown in the belt project in Figures 4–15c–h.

When you have finished wrapping your core, thread the yarn end through a blunt yarn needle. Stitch the end through the last few winds, and then trim the core to the desired length. If you prefer not to have the core showing, however, Figure 4–12 shows some alternate ways to end a wrapped element. Figure

4–11 Festival ornament. Barbara Chapman. 40"
high. Multiple elements, including yarn
wrapped over ready-made baskets, figure 8
wrapping, pom-poms, tassels and a small ojo
de Dios.

4–12 Sample wrapped cords and endings.

4–13 is a good example of how the ending technique can be used as an integral part of the piece.

NO-CORE WRAPPING

In truth, there is a core in no-core wrapping. This technique is called "no-core" wrapping because the core materials are the wrapping yarns. All yarns are interchangeable. In other words, any yarn can be pulled from the core to wrap around the other yarns. By the same token, any yarn that is not wrapping becomes part of the core.

Changing yarns is especially easy in no-core wrapping. That ease is a major advantage for artists who wish frequent changes in color and texture. Also the multiple strands make it possible to create yarn beads and to alternate simple wrapping with split wrapping and figure 8 wrapping.

MAKING A BELT

No-core wrapping with all the special effects is shown in the sample belt project shown in Figure 4–14. As in basic wrapping, follow the photographs if you are right-handed. To be precise, hold the core yarns in your left hand and the wrapping yarn in your right hand.

4–13 Untitled. Jon Riis. Section of fiber construction. Total size: 9′6″ x 32′6″. Montage of wrapped tassels on a handwoven backing. Wool yarns with brass wrappings near the tassels. Beige through greys; yellow through brick orange-red. Photographed at the Los Angeles Bonaventure Hotel.

To begin, cut several 4-foot lengths of cord. In the belt shown, there are twenty-five 4-foot lengths of shiny rayon. These 4-foot lengths are starting cords. Whenever you use up a cord, add another 4-foot length. In this way, the width of the core remains consistent. Do not worry if the cords are uneven in length. You can trim them when you are finished wrapping.

Starting the Belt

To start the belt, lay the wrapping yarn against the core fibers near one end. Wind toward the end. Keep winding until you are about ½″ from the end (Fig. 4–15a).

Make a loop by folding in the wrapped end (Fig. 4–15b). Wind yarn around all core materials. The result is a large loop that is wrapped with yarn. Continue to wrap yarn around the core fibers. Switch wrapping yarns to change colors. Add a new 4-foot length of yarn each time you use up a wrapping yarn.

Split Wrapping and Figure 8 Wrapping

Split wrapping and figure 8 wrapping are variations on the simple wrapping method. Both techniques convert a single wrapped element into two thinner wrapped elements. Split wrapping and figure 8 wrapping are possible with any multistrand core. Take a look at Barbara Chapman's ornament in Figure 4–11 which features figure 8 wrappings among other wrapped elements.

Figure 4–15c shows the start of the split wrapping technique. Separate core materials into two equal groups. Hold one group aside, and wrap the other group with the wrapping yarn. Knot the end temporarily and put the wrapped group aside. Using any yarn from the unwrapped group, wrap remaining yarns. In Figure 4–15d, the two wrapped groups have been twisted together for added depth and interest.

Figures 4–15e through 4–15h show figure 8 wrapping where the fibers are divided into two equal groups and the wrapping yarn is carried under the left side (Fig. 4–15e), over the left side (Fig. 4–15f), under the right side (Fig. 4–15g) and over the right side (Fig. 4–15h). This sequence is repeated until your figure 8 wrapping is the desired length.

4–14 The completed wrapped belt, using yarn beads, split wrapping and figure 8 techniques, is finished with closed buckle and trimmed tassel.

4–15a Starting the belt.

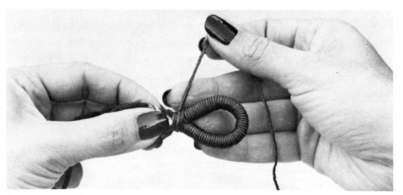

4–15b Folding in the wrapped end.

4–15c Split wrapping technique.

4-15d Holding both groups of split wrapping together, use any yarn to wrap all cords together.

4-15e For figure 8 wrapping, separate core fibers into two equal groups. Take the wrapping yarn under the left side.

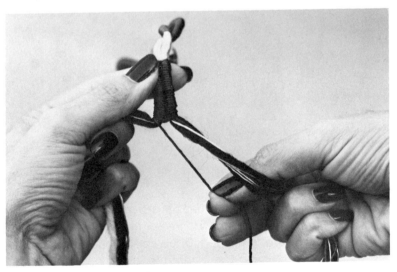

4-15f Take it over the left side.

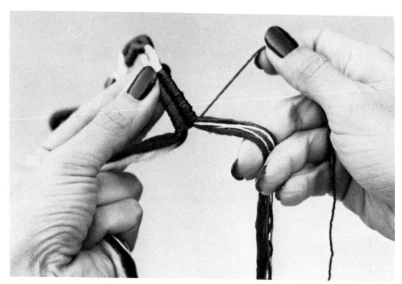

4–15g Now, under the right side.

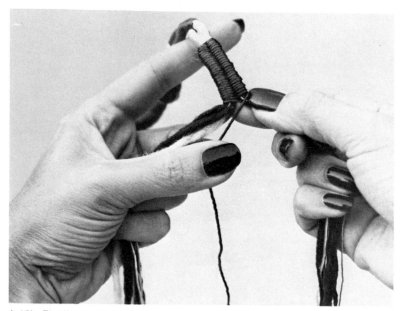

4–15h Finally, over the right side.

Yarn Beads

Yarn beads look like beads that have been strung along the wrapped elements (Fig. 4–15c). However, the beads are actually built-up areas of yarn. A network of yarns in a contrasting color holds each bead in place. The technique for making yarn beads is illustrated in Figure 4–16.

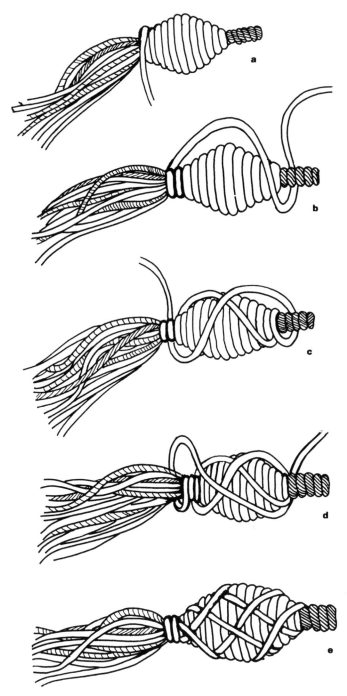

4–16 Making yarn beads.

To make the beads, hold the original wrapping yarn against the core. Using a second color of yarn, wrap the same area over and over again until you build up a mound (Fig. 4–16a). Hold the second color of yarn against the core. Using a third

4–18 *(Opposite page)* Wrapped necklace. Robin Brisco. Wrapped elements over stone slices. Joined with invisible thread. Note button clasp and figure 8 stitching near the top. Beige silk yarns on linen core. Photograph by Chet Brisco.

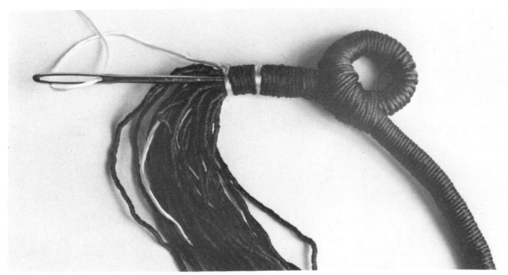

4–17 Making a buckle.

color of yarn, wrap the core twice and bring the yarn to the other side of the bead (Fig. 4–16b). Wrap the core and bring the yarn back over the bead (Fig. 4–16c). Wrap the core again and bring the yarn over the bead, beneath the last line of yarn (Fig. 4–16d). Repeat the process until the bead is wrapped in a network of yarns (Fig. 4–16e).

Finishing the Belt

Belts are interesting projects for no-core wrapping. No matter how small, or large, your waist, you can always plan or add enough length for yarn beads, figure 8's, split wrappings and color changes. When you are satisfied with the belt, the last step is ending it. The finished belt shown in Figure 4–14 ends with a simple buckle and hanging tassel.

Making a Buckle

To make a buckle, measure your waist. Wrap the core with fibers until your belt is 3″ larger than your waist measurement. Loop the last 3″ into a circle. Wrap the circle and core together, and keep wrapping for an inch or two. Thread the end through a yarn needle and stitch through the last few winds (Fig. 4–17).

Figure 4–18 shows how the same techniques used for this belt can be applied to make a wrapped necklace.

75 WRAPPING

BRAIDING: MORE THAN A LANYARD

One night, very late, hanging a new basket seemed important. A plain cord wasn't good enough, and unless I flew to another time zone, I couldn't expect to find a store open. So before cutting off a length of leather lacing, I turned to the yarns in my workroom. That's when I rediscovered braiding. After some experimenting with different yarns, I found myself with a 4-strand braid.

Braiding is easy, as I re-learned that night. It is also remarkably enjoyable. Even though I hadn't braided anything but pigtails in years, my fingers seemed to work automatically, with hardly a moment's thought. You may not realize it, but you probably know how to make a 4-strand braid too.

Everyone knows the 3-strand braid. That braid is used for children's pigtails. A 3-strand braid is the simplest form of braiding. Most of us can make 3-strand braids with our eyes closed. Four-strand braids are almost as familiar to many of us. Probably every former camper took home a few 4-strand braids at the end of the summer. We called them "lanyards" then. Lanyards were invariably keychains, whistle-holders or a combination of the two. And they were always two colors of shining plastic.

For parents, these 4-strand braids were wonderful gifts. Counselors blessed their time-consuming nature. "Give the kids lanyards," they probably thought. "It'll keep them out of trouble for hours." And it did. Campers loved the repetitive, almost mesmerizing motion. With very little thought, four separate cords soon turned into a functional, attractive braid.

Braids were enjoyable to make then, and they are equally enjoyable today. If we think beyond lanyards, the same techniques can produce exciting results. Braids may be made with any fiber and any number of cords. Besides braids for their own sake, belts, hanging cords, handbags and wall pieces are all possible.

Braiding has a long history throughout the world. This chapter explores some sample braids, and shows examples of braided projects. Take a look through this chapter for ideas. Try the different braids with whatever fibers you have on hand. Then someday if you're ever confronted with a basket you want to hang, you'll know exactly what to do.

5–1 Construction #1. Libby Conway.
Three-strand braids stand out on a
multimethod hanging. Other fiber techniques
include macrame, Ghiordes knots and fabric
stretched over cardboard circles. Wools and
cotton mopcord.

THE BRAIDING OR FINGERWEAVING PROCESS

Sometimes braiding is referred to as *fingerweaving.* This term describes the process perfectly. Your fingers are the tools, and they weave the yarns together. There are no looms, shuttles, beaters or even needles to weave with. Also unlike other forms of weaving, there are no separate *warp* or *weft* yarns. In traditional weaving, the weft yarns weave under and over the fixed warp yarns. Throughout most braids, on the other hand, the warp yarns take turns acting as the weft.

This chapter explores flat braids and round braids with four or more strands. The thickness of a braid, however, has nothing to do with whether it is a 4-strand or 40-strand braid. A little girl's pigtail, for example, is a 3-strand braid, yet each "strand" consists of countless hairs. In the same way, each strand in a braid can be any number of yarns. Feel free to use large groups of fibers in each working strand.

In this chapter, the word *strand* always means the working strand, no matter how many cords it consists of. Also, to eliminate confusion, only the word "braiding" is used to describe the actual braiding, or fingerweaving, process.

MATERIALS

The modern braider has an enormous selection of fibers to choose from. That selection includes almost any flexible, natural or synthetic fiber. Smooth yarns with little or no stretch are easiest to work with. As a consequence, cotton, linen and rayon yarns are popular for braids. These fibers are especially well-suited to belts, cords and neckchains.

Wool, silk, jute, sisal and novelty yarns are also appropriate for some braids. Highly textured and bulky yarns work well in large pieces. Thin yarns are good for delicate braids. Heavy yarns are best for first projects. Yarns pull together as you braid, and the result might be far slimmer than you expect.

All yarns in your braid do not have to be of the same fiber. However, if your yarns stretch at all, be sure they have the same amount of elasticity. Choose as many colors as you like. Colors blend together beautifully in a braid. Watching the colors move along as you braid is one of the joys of the craft. From time to time, even veteran braiders find surprises in the patterns that develop.

Although a core is not necessary, it is sometimes desirable. A core makes a round braid thicker and prevents the braid from stretching. Jute, sisal, linen, cotton or any other nonstretch fibers work well as core materials.

Sample braids shown throughout this chapter are made with Lily Mills Macra-Cord.

BASIC PRINCIPLES

The same principles apply to round and flat braids. These principles are discussed below. Read them before you start your braid. If you are a beginner, try a 4-strand braid first. As soon as the basic technique is mastered, it is simple to learn the more complicated, multiple-strand braids.

Tension

Uniform tension is vital in braiding. In general, a tight braid is preferable to a loose one. More important, however, is maintaining the same tension throughout the braid. Don't feel frustrated if your first few braids seem uneven. It takes time to develop the steady pattern and rhythm that results in an even-looking braid with a straight edge and even slant to all the cords.

As a guide to making an even braid, you'll want to periodically measure the width and the number of horizontal cords per inch. This will help regulate the tension so it's not too tight or too loose.

To keep tension in the cords, secure the ends to a fixed object. Use whatever seems convenient. Hang the braid on a nail,

5–2 Festival Ornament. Barbara Chapman. 34″ high. Eight-strand round braid crowned by a brass butterfly and wrapped cords. Braided of handspun wool and wool-wrapped cords.

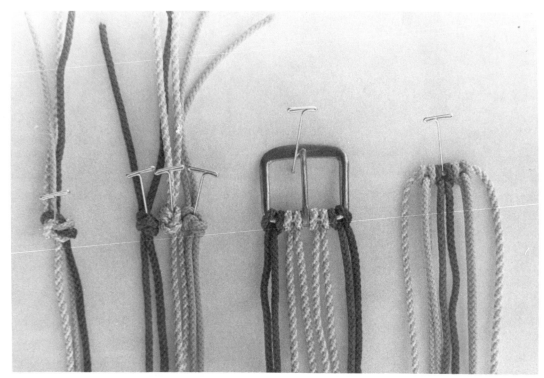

5–3 Sample starting methods for braiding. Left to right, knotted ends for a round braid; knotted ends for a flat braid; reverse lark's head knot on buckle; reverse lark's head knot on braiding cord.

5–4 Belt. 2″ wide. Twenty-four-strand flat braid, ending in four 6-strand braids. Synthetic yarns. Rust, deep brown and white.

doorknob or hook; clamp the braid into a clipboard, drawer or vise; or pin it to a macrame board.

Tangling

From time to time, cords get tangled. Tangling is inevitable in braiding. Whenever you are faced with an intertwined mass of cords, pull one cord from the group. Most often all cords will loosen as a result. To prevent especially long cords from tangling, roll the ends into center-pull balls as shown in Figure 4–5. Use rubber bands to secure each ball, and let cord out as the braid progresses.

Starting a Braid

There are a few different ways to start braids, depending upon how you'd like the top edge to look. Some sample beginnings are shown in Figure 5–3.

To start a braid, cut the cords to size. Determining the proper length is not simple. The amount needed increases with the number of strands, the tension of the weave, the addition of a core and the starting method. The guidelines below apply to a typical 4-strand braid without a core.

For a knotted end, cut each cord one-and-a-half to two times the length you desire for the finished braid. Tie the ends in a knot. Don't make the knots too near the ends. That way, you can untie the knots later and turn them into tassels or smaller braids.

As an alternative to the knotted edge, start on a buckle, ring, twig or other object. For this starting method, cut cords three to four times the length you desire for the finished braid. Then double each yarn, and tie them to the object with a reverse lark's head knot as shown in Figure 7–10.

For a flat edge, substitute one of the braiding cords for the buckle, ring, twig or other object. Lay the cord on the work area in a horizontal position. In knotting, this horizontal cord is called a *holding* cord. Using a reverse lark's head knot, tie all other cords to the midpoint of this holding cord. When you braid the cords together, incorporate the holding cord into the braid.

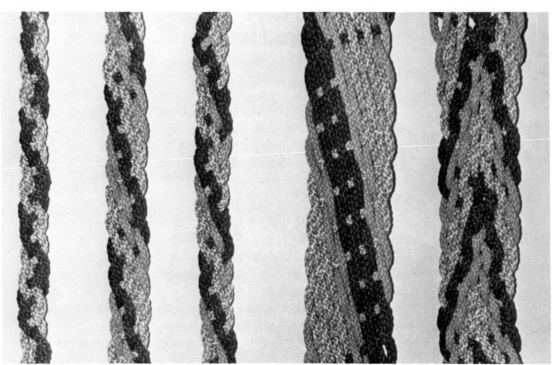

5–5 Sample flat braids. Left to right, 4-strand braid; 5-strand braid; 6-strand braid; 12-strand braid; 12-strand chevron braid.

FLAT BRAIDS

Flat braids are perfect for belts, handbags and decorative trims. They are particularly simple and therefore a good way for beginners to learn braiding. As you'll see, flat braids are easy in any width, with any number of cords. Some sample flat braids are shown in Figure 5–5. Step-by-step instructions and illustrations follow.

Four-Strand

Figure 5-6 shows how to make a 4-strand flat braid. Bring the left cord over the cord to its right (Fig. 5–6a). Bring the right cord under the cord to its immediate left, and over the next

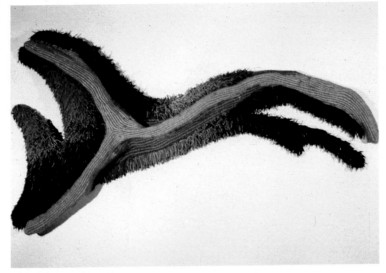

Untitled. Libby Platus. 9′x3′x1′. Cross-tension knotting in sisal and Maxi-cord. Leather Ghiordes knots. Photographed at Security Pacific Bank, South Pasadena, CA. Photo courtesy of the author.

Have You Been to Haunama Bay? Libby Platus. 6′x4′x1½′. Cross-tension knotting. Sisal and Maxi-cord. Discovery Bay, Hawaii. Photograph courtesy of the author.

Cisza III. Kris Dey. 20'x10'. Fabric strips wrapped on PVC tubes. Photograph courtesy of the author.

Bopus. Kris Dey. Detail of wrapping piece. Photograph courtesy of the author.

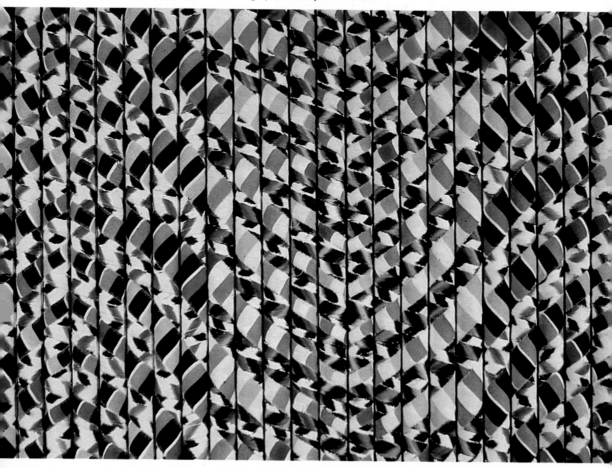

(*Above*) Ode to C. G. Adams Jr. Joan Michaels-Paque. Hitching. Synthetic fibers. Collection of Connie Nicoud, Oregon. Photograph by Henry P. Paque.

(*Right*) Conical Hanging Basket. Mary Ann York. 12″ high; 10″ diameter. Ermine tails, shells and tin cones decorate this coiled basket. Goat hair and camel hair. Photograph by Rich Tardif.

(*Left*) Untitled. Nan Hackett Joe. Coiling and weaving. Wools and novelty yarns. Photograph courtesy of the artist.

Sisal Fence. Susan Nelson. 18″x26″. Hand-dyed chenille over sisal. Photograph by Steven Nelson.

Root Basket. Nan Hacket Joe. 24″ high. Protruding roots act as the warp in a twined basket. Handspun wool. Photographed at the Rusty Needle, Laguna Beach, CA.

(*Above*) Coiled basket. Ellen Appel. 6″ high, 9″
diameter. Predominantly figure 8 stitching in Stanley
Berroco's Nature Wool and Nubs 'n Slubs. Imbricated
with Homespun. Lily basketry core.

Coiled basket. Janet Ennis. 8″ high; 6″ diameter.
Imbricated basket, decorated with beads, coconut
hishi and contrasting coils. Wool and novelty yarns.

(*Right*) Frog basket. Sharon La Pierre. 18″ high.
Figure 8 coiling; crocheted details. Wool yarns.
Photograph courtesy of the artist.

(*Left*) Overlapping Circles. Joan Michaels-Paque. 3′ long. Hitching. Synthetic fibers. Collection of Connie Nicoud, Oregon. Photograph by Henry P. Paque.

(*Below*) Circle weaving. Ellen Appel. 14″ diameter. Wools and novelty yarns. Predominantly a plain weave with leno and soumak details.

Facing page:
(*Above*) Wrapped belts. Ellen Appel. No-core wrappings in shiny rayons.

(*Below left*) Ojo de Dios. Basic wrap, wing wrap and star wrap in alternating colors. Framed in basic wrap and star wrap. 2-ply wool.

(*Below right*) Coiled wall hanging. Mary Ann York. 22″ high; 10″ diameter. Figure 8 stitching. Mohair and other looped yarns. Photograph by Rich Tardif.

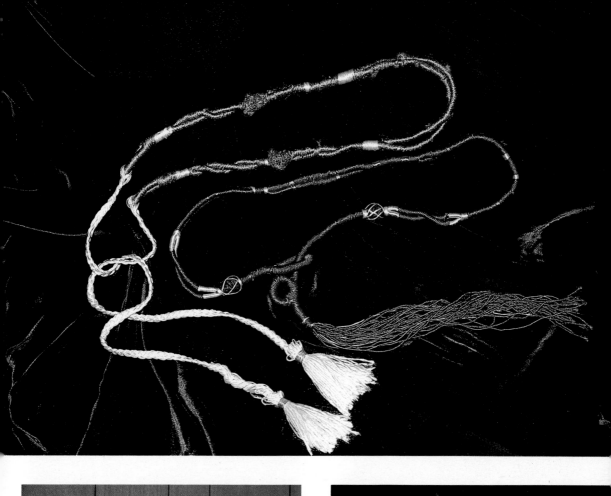

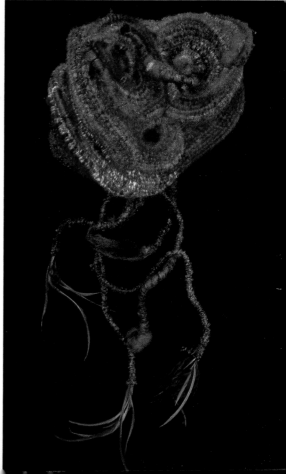

Two yarnpaintings in the series "Six Stages of the Transformation of the Sun" by José Benitez Sanchez. Photograph courtesy of Gilman Galleries, Chicago.

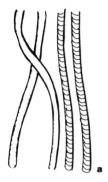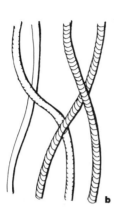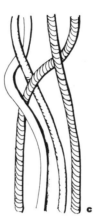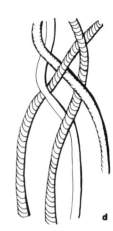

5–6 Making a 4-strand flat braid.

cord to the left (Fig. 5–6b). Repeat these steps throughout the braid. Figures 5–6c and 5–6d show how the next row looks.

With Odd Numbers of Cords

To make a flat braid with an odd number of cords, bring the left cord over the cord to its right (Fig. 5–7). Hold the new left cord apart from the rest (Fig. 5–7a). Starting with an *over* motion, weave the right cord through the other cords (Fig. 5–7b). Repeat these steps throughout the braid. Figures 5–7c and 5–7d show how the next row looks.

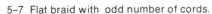

5–7 Flat braid with odd number of cords.

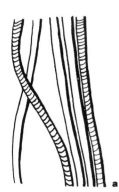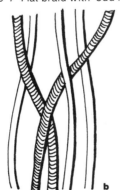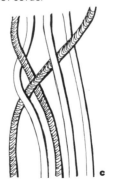

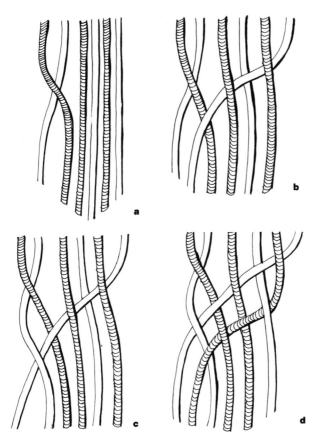

5–8 Flat braid with even number of cords.

With Even Numbers of Cords

For a flat braid with an even number of cords, bring the left cord *over* the cord to its right (Fig. 5–8). Hold the new left cord apart from the rest (Fig. 5–8a). Starting with an *under* motion, weave the right cord through the other cords (Fig. 5–8b). Repeat these steps throughout the braid. Figures 5–8c and 5–8d show how the next row looks.

Chevron Flat Braids

Figure 5–9 shows how to make a chevron flat braid with an odd number of cords. Divide the cords into two groups. Put the extra cord in the left group. Starting with an *over* motion,

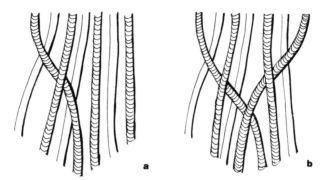

5–9 Chevron flat braid with odd number of cords.

weave the left cord through the left group and place it alongside the right cords (Fig. 5–9a). Starting with an *over* motion,
weave the right cord through the right group. This now includes the original left cord (Fig 5–9b). Repeat these steps
throughout the braid.

To make a chevron flat braid with an even number of cords,
divide the cords into two groups (Fig. 5–10). Starting with an
over motion, weave the left cord through the left group and
place it alongside the right group (Fig. 5–10a). Starting with an
under motion, weave the far right cord through the right group
which now includes the original left cord (Fig. 5–10b). Repeat
these steps throughout the braid.

5–10 Chevron flat braid with even number of cords.

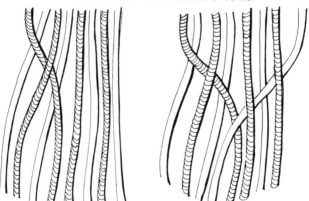

ROUND BRAIDS

Round braids make beautiful neckchains and decorative cords. (Figs. 5–11 and 5–12). I always need a cord of some kind. Either I'm replacing a cord on a handbag, suspending something from the ceiling or restringing a wonderful old pendant from the Swap Meet. Round braids are always the perfect solution. Four-strand, 6-strand and 8-strand round braids are illustrated in Figure 5–13. If you wish to have a thick braid, either work the strands around a core or use several cords for each working strand.

Four-Strand

To make the 4-strand round braid as shown in Figure 5–14, bring the left cord over the center two cords, and back under the center-right cord (Fig. 5–14a). Bring the right cord over the center two cords, and back under the center-left cord (Fig. 5–14b). Repeat these steps throughout the braid. Figures 5–14c and 5–14d show how the next row looks.

Six-Strand

To make the 6-strand round braid as shown in Figure 5–15, divide the cords into two groups of three cords. Bring the left cord under all cords. Then bring it over, under and over the right cords, and place it alongside the left cords (Fig. 5–15a). Bring the right cord under all cords. Then bring it over, under and over the left cords, which now includes the original left cord (Fig. 5–15b). Repeat these steps with the new left and right cords.

Eight-Strand

To make the 8-strand round braid as shown in Figure 5–16, divide the cords into two groups of four cords. Bring the left cord under all other cords. Then bring it over, under, over and under the right cords, and place it alongside the left cords (Fig. 5–16a). Bring the right cord under all other cords. Then bring it over, under, over and under the left cords, which now includes the original left cord (Fig. 5–16b). Repeat these steps with the new left and right cords.

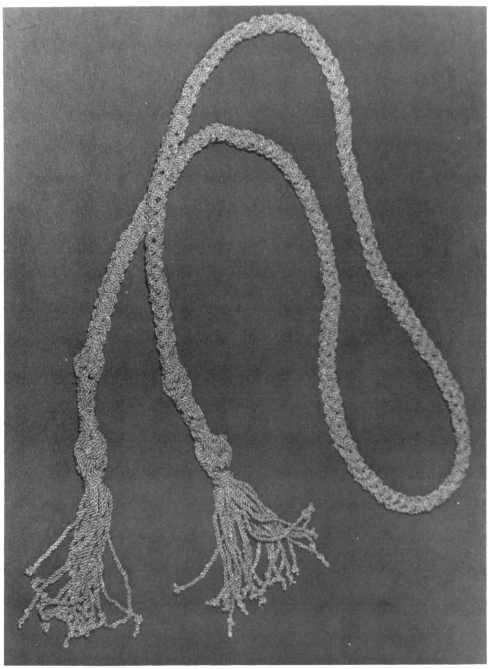

5–11 Belt. 50″ long. Six-strand round braid in 2-ply rayon. Braided on a jute core, with 2 yarns in each strand.

5–12 Three-strand and 8-strand braided cords with pendants. Both braided in shiny novelty cords.

5–13 Sample round braids. Left to right, 4-strand braid; 6-strand braid; 8-strand braid; 6-strand braid over jute core.

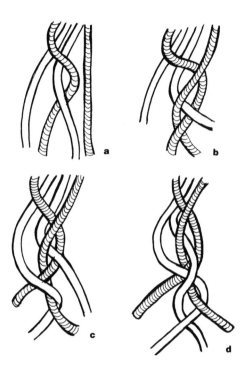

5–14 Making a 4-strand
round braid.

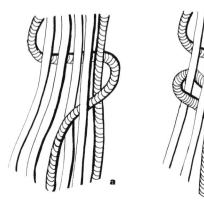

5–15 Making a 6-strand
round braid.

5–17 Bellhanger. 32″ long. System of braids in varying thicknesses. Divided and regrouped into different-size braids throughout. All Stanley Berroco yarns including Homespun, Bim Bam, Nature Wool, Dji Dji and Que Linda. Shades of blue and gold.

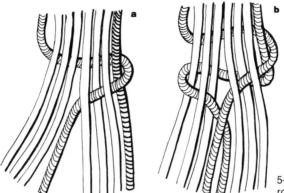

5–16 Making an 8-strand round braid.

SPLICING CORDS

If you run out of cord as you're braiding, there are two ways to add a new cord. One method is to untwist the ends of both cords and then twist both ends together. If needed, add a tiny dab of glue. As an alternate method, lay the new cord alongside the original cord. Let the ends overlap for a few inches, and work both ends as though they were one cord. Never add cords at an outer edge. The best place to add new cords is at the center of the braid.

VARIATIONS IN BRAIDING

Besides making regular, even braids, it is also possible to change the shape of a braid. To change shape, divide the braid into smaller braids. Later you can rejoin the cords or divide them into even smaller units.

To make an especially wide braid, make smaller interlinking units. By interlinking flat braids, there is no limit to the width that is possible. The technique for interlinking braids is shown in Figure 5–18.

INTERLINKING BRAIDS

To interlink two braids, work the left braid as usual. For the right braid, loop the left cord over and under the right cord in the left braid. Then work the right braid as usual.

95 BRAIDING

5–19 Persian Piece. Karen Chapnick. 5′ x 8′. System of interlocking braids. Hand-dyed sisal. Pale shades of blues, grays, and turquoise; dark shades of brown and black; framed in multiple shades of red. Rayon wrappings. Photograph courtesy of the artist.

Figure 5–18 shows how to interlink two braids. However, any number of braids may be interlinked the same way (Fig. 5–19).

ENDING A BRAID

Take a look at Figure 5–20; it shows several ways to end a braid. A discussion of each method follows.

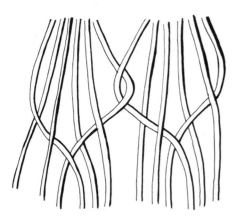

5–18 Interlinking braids.

5–20 Sample ending methods for braids. Left to right, overhand knot on round braid; overhand knots on flat braid; wrapping on unplied ends; multiple braid wrapped ending.

One of the best and simplest ways to end a braid is to knot the ends. In round braids, tie all ends together into one knot. In flat braids, divide cords into small groups and knot each group with an overhand knot as shown in Figure 7–11.

For another easy ending, substitute a wrapping cord for the overhand knot. The short wrap, appropriate for the braided ends, is described in Figure 4–10.

Whether you wrap or tie the ends, hanging cords are often more interesting as a frizzy tassel. To make the tassel, separate plied cords into each individual ply. Fluff up the plies and trim the ends.

5–21 Playground for a Woman. Libby Platus. Section of self-supported structure of braided rawhide. Total size: 8' x 7' x 6". Photograph courtesy of the artist.

One last method for ending a braid is with more braids. To braid the ends, divide the original braid into smaller units. Braid each group separately, and then end with an overhand knot or wrapping cord.

MAGIC YARNCRAFTS: FROM THE HUICHOL INDIANS

6–1 Yarnpainting. Depicts the birth of the Mother of Gods, incorporating the ocean and land. From the collection of Loren and Toshi Kajitani.

I wish I could tell you about the time I watched the Huichol Indians create fabulous yarnpaintings and ojos de Dios (*eye of God*). I can't, however, because I've never visited their settlements in Mexico. As much as I'd enjoy the adventure, the Huicholes live in a remote, inaccessible region of Mexico, in the high mountains of the West Central Sierra Madre. A visit requires a journey of several days. The steep slopes and deep canyons along the way make the trip literally impossible during the rainy season. Their home is almost as difficult to reach today as it was centuries ago. The only difference is that nowadays, dirt runways allow limited access by private plane.

6–2 Yarnpainting. *Peyoteras,* or peyote hunters, on a pilgrimage to gather the plants. Photographed at A Touch of Latin, Laguna Beach, CA.

6–3 Yarnpainting. Head of the sacred deer. Vibrant tones on hot pink. Photographed at A Touch of Latin, Laguna Beach, CA.

6–4 Yarnpainting. Represents the peyote blossom. Predominantly blue. Photographed at A Touch of Latin, Laguna Beach, CA.

Because of this almost total isolation, the Huicholes remain nearly untouched by the modern world. Huichol beliefs, customs and rituals survived even the Spanish conquistadores. Like their ancestors, the Huicholes grow crops, hunt for food and pray to Gods of nature. Their religion is ancient. It is based on myth and magic, and dates back to Mexican prehistory.

One important ritual concerns the gathering of peyote. This hallucinatory plant is important to the Huichol religion. It appears in artwork and legend over and over again, as you can see from the yarnpaintings throughout this chapter. Each year, Huichol holy men lead a 300-mile pilgrimage to *Wirikuta,* the sacred land in San Luis Potosi where peyote grows. At the fields, *peyoteras* capture the plant with bow and arrow, and then begin the long journey home.

The yarncrafts, like the peyote hunt, are part of religious ritual. These crafts are a way of communicating with the Gods. Yarnpaintings are a prayer in picture form; ojos de Dios are eyes through which the Gods watch over their followers. The brilliant colors and exotic designs make these crafts a unique source of exploration for the modern fiberartist.

Maybe those adventurers among you will journey to Huichol territory for the first-hand look at their beautiful handcrafts. For the rest of us who want to learn the techniques anyway, this chapter presents the basic instructions for yarnpaintings and ojos de Dios.

YARNPAINTING

Authentic Huichol yarnpaintings are wonderfully intricate and brilliant in color. Probably the most descriptive, albeit vintage, word for them is *psychedelic.* Traditional works are *painted* with strands of yarn and presented to the gods.

Yarnpaintings tell a story in pictures and symbols. They relate myths, ritual and religious visions. Some symbols, themes and characterizations recur in Huichol yarnpaintings. The peyote deer, peyote blossoms, serpents and many of the nature gods appear frequently. The peyote hunt also appears in Hui-

6–5 Yarnpainting. People, animals and bumblebees. Photographed at the Red Onion Restaurant, Lido, Newport Beach, CA.

chol yarnpaintings. Many yarnpaintings, in fact, are a result of peyote-inspired visions.

Nonreligious paintings show people, flowers, birds and other everyday subjects. However, in the hands of a skilled Huichol artist, even the most ordinary subjects look far from commonplace.

Classic yarnpainting requires beeswax and a warm sun to work in. To paint with yarn, the Huichol spreads wax onto a wooden board and scratches a design into the wax. He then presses yarn along the outlines, spiraling the yarn into the figures and backgrounds. The warm sun keeps the wax soft until the board is completely filled with vibrant yarns.

This chapter presents a simplified method of yarnpainting. Instead of beeswax and a warm sun, commercial glue acts as a substitute.

6–6 First painting in a series: Six Stages of the Transformation of the Sun I by José Benitez Sanchez. The Suns Opens His Path in the Underworld. The mouth of the rock: the first step. Represents the sun's journey into the underworld as it plunges into the west beneath the ocean. The sun's day path is represented by a white serpent (left). The night path is a blue serpent (right). Great Grandfather "Tatutsi Xuweri Timaiweme" stands at the center, with Father Sun seated at his left and Grandfather Fire seated on his right. The arrow (top left) is Father Sun as he slides into the underworld and plants himself in an altar (lower right). The flowers are the trail of dew and water. Dispersed dots represent the words exchanged by the gods. Photograph courtesy of Gilman Galleries, Chicago.

Materials

Wool yarns are best for yarn painting. Wool tends to expand and fill in unavoidable tiny spaces. Two-ply, 3-ply or 4-ply carpet yarns are suggested. Avoid heavy yarns, handspun yarns, novelty yarns and anything highly textured. For a small painting, two or three ounces are sufficient. Use yarn scraps for accent colors. Include black for borders and outlines.

Besides yarn, you'll need Masonite, particle board or plywood for the backing. Also, the process requires rubber cement or a tacky glue for applying the yarn. If you don't have a long fingernail, you'll also need a long nail or other pointed implement.

Drawing a Design

Choose any subject for your yarnpainting. Make the design as complex or as simple as you like, but eliminate shading and tiny details. Draw large outlined areas for solid sections of yarn. Before it is filled with yarn, the design should resemble a page from a child's coloring book.

If you don't wish to draw your own pattern, coloring books, in truth, are perfect for yarnpainting. Many intricate and sophisticated coloring books are available for adults today in subjects from butterflies to intergalactic space travel. Copy any design onto your board, or transfer a picture with carbon paper. At that point, you are ready to begin *painting* with yarn.

Starting the Yarnpainting

Coat the outline of your backboard with glue. Twist the end of the yarn, and press two or three rows of black yarn along the outer border. Apply one line of yarn along main outlines of your design (Fig. 6–7a). Use tacky glue or wait for rubber cement to become tacky before *painting* with yarns.

Filling in Shapes

To fill in shapes, apply glue just inside the outline of one shape. Fill in the shape with yarn. Place each new line of yarn as close to the previous line as possible. To get into corners

6–7a Starting the yarnpainting by outlining the design along the border.

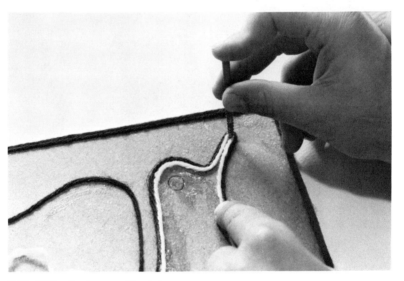

6–7b Filling in shapes with yarn.

and slim spaces, turn the yarn around your fingernail, a long nail or other pointed implement (Fig. 6–7b).

Add glue and new lines of yarn until the lines meet to form smaller shapes (Fig. 6–7c). Fill in tiny details, such as eyes, as you reach them.

107 MAGIC YARNCRAFTS

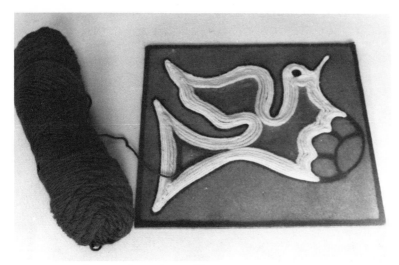

6–7c Keep adding new lines of yarn. Fill in tiny details, such as eyes, as you reach them.

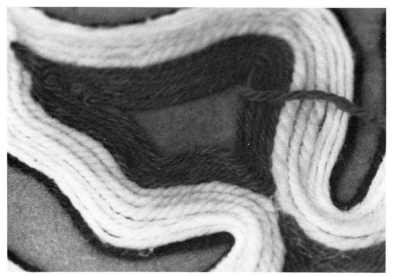

6–7d As the yarn lines become smaller and smaller, take special care to define all curves carefully, using same or different colors.

Fill in smaller shapes with the same or different colors. As the yarn lines become smaller and smaller, take special care to define all curves carefully (Fig. 6–7d).

Filling in the Background

The final step is to add a few lines of yarn inside the border and around each shape. Fill in the remaining background areas one small section at a time (Fig. 6–7e).

6–7e Fill in the remaining background areas one small section at a time.

OJO DE DIOS

Ojo de Dios translates as *eye of God.* The Huichol Indians make these brilliant symbols so that the Gods may watch over them. Ojos are formed by stretching yarns over crossed sticks. The *eye* itself is a dark-colored, diamond shape at the center. It is through this eye that the Gods view their followers.

Huichol fathers create ojos for each child. Since the mortality rate is high among children, the Huicholes call upon the Gods to see them through their early years. Each year, fathers add another eye symbol until the child is five years old.

Traditional ojos de Dios never have more than five eyes. Modern fiberartists, however, are free to make ojos in any size, colors and with any number of yarns. The examples that follow include a variety of decorative ojos. The simplest ojo de Dios is made with two crossed sticks. This version is the 4-arm ojo. Figures 6–10 and 6–11 show how to make a 4-arm ojo with a variety of wrapping methods.

Materials

Use plied or unplied yarns for ojos de Dios. Knitting yarn and carpet yarn are popular. For unusual effects, try novelty yarns, metallic threads or variegated yarns. Avoid handspuns, extra-heavy yarns, high textures, "thick and thin" yarns and non-stretch fibers like linen and jute. Use bright colors, earth tones or a combination of both. If you have yarn scraps left from other projects, use them as accent colors. One or two-ounce

6–8 Multicolored 8-arm ojo de Dios, using basic wrap, wing wrap and star wrap in alternating colors. Framed in basic wrap and star wrap. 2-ply wool. Collection of Janet Ennis.

6–9 Multicolored 8-arm ojo de Dios, with alternating basic wrap and star wrap. Short wings at center. Novelty yarns from Stanley Berroco, including Homespun and Que Linda.

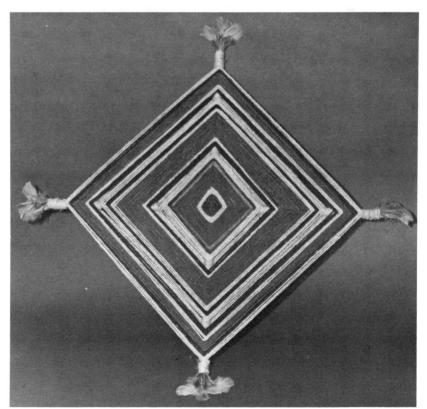

6–10 Four-arm ojo de Dios, using basic wrap and back wrap. This one ends with a feather on each arm. Homespun from Stanley Berroco and Nature Wool.

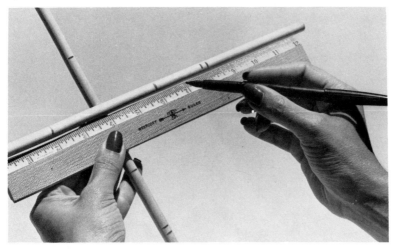

6–11a Preparing the dowel frame for wrapping.

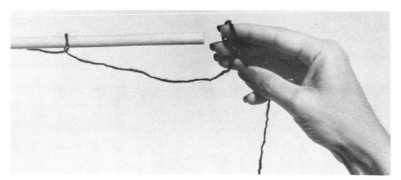

6–11b Starting to wrap with a double half-hitch on each arm.

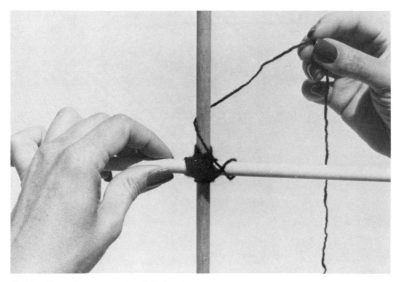

6–11c Form the eye, using this basic wrap.

balls in three colors are more than enough for an 18″, 4-arm ojo.

For the frame, get two 18″ dowels in ¹/₄″ or ³/₈″ diameters. Dowels are available in 36″ lengths at most building supply stores and lumberyards. For larger ojos, choose dowels with ¹/₄″ diameters. Besides yarn and dowels, other needed supplies are white glue, a ruler, marking pen and utility knife. If you plan to sketch your ojo in advance, you'll also need paper and colored marking pens.

In the project that follows, you'll see novelty yarns from Stanley Berroco. They include Homespun in two earth tones and white Nature Wool.

Starting the Ojo

The first step is to make the frame. To start, notch each dowel with a utility knife. Very carefully make deep notches at the center of each dowel. Then glue dowels together with white glue. Check to be sure dowels form perfect right angles. Let glue dry.

To sketch a design beforehand, draw the design in colors that correspond to your yarns. When the frame is ready, mark the arms wherever your design calls for changes in colors and wrapping methods (Fig. 6–11a). Feel free to change your design as you go along. As you wrap, your yarns will cover the markings. Therefore no design decision at this stage is irreversible.

To start the wrapping, make a double half-hitch (as shown in Fig. 7–13) on each arm. Like "casting on" in knitting, make each loop on your finger and slip it on the dowel (Fig. 6–11b).

Basic Wrapping

The procedure for basic wrapping is to pass the yarn over and under each arm. Pull yarn taut, and push the loop toward the center. Form the *eye* using this basic wrap (Fig. 6–11c).

Various Wrapping Methods

There are two ways to wrap an ojo. Either move counterclockwise from arm to arm, or *twirl* the yarn onto the frame.

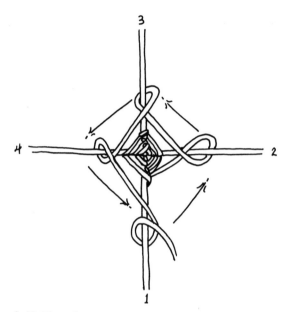

6–12 Wrapping counterclockwise.

Use whichever method feels most comfortable to you. As a general rule, ojo-makers prefer twirling as the wrappings become larger.

Starting from the bottom arm, move from arm to arm, wrapping in a counterclockwise direction (Fig. 6–12). This method is best for small ojos de Dios and the early stages of larger ojos.

Twirling is the best method when ojos become larger (Fig. 6–13). With twirling, it is less awkward to wrap the ojo, and easier to control the tension. Hold arm 1 in your left hand. Hold yarn in your right hand. Wrap yarn over arm 2 (Fig. 6–13a). Turn ojo to the back (Fig. 6–13b). Move your left hand to arm 2, and turn ojo around to the front (Fig. 6–13c). Repeat this procedure with each arm in sequence.

Tension

Proper tension is important in ojos. Keep yarn taut as you wrap, and always push the loops you form toward the center of

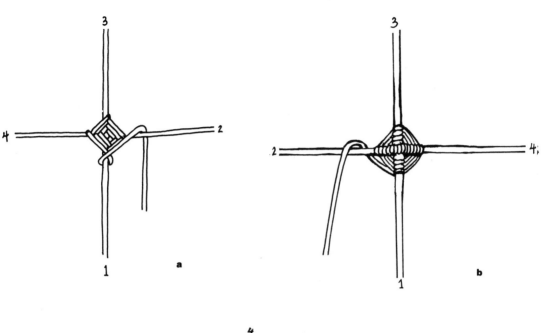

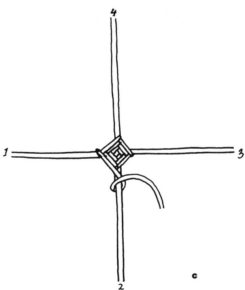

6–13 Twirling.

6–14 Star ojo. Central star wrappings surrounded by wings. Two-ply knitting yarns from Coats & Clark, including Red Heart Shetland Look, Texture Delight and Wintuk Sport Yarn. Predominantly gray and beige, outlined in red.

6–15 Double ojo. Asymmetrical shapes formed by space wrapping. Back wrap in dark red creates recessed area behind the eyes. Predominantly beige. Novelty yarns from Stanley Berroco, including Homespun, Nubs 'n Slubs and Mirabella.

the ojo. From time to time, dab glue on the wrapped dowels in back of the ojo. The glue prevents wrappings from slackening later. If the yarn bunches up as you wrap, add extra loops as you wrap each arm. Unless you desire an asymmetrical effect, give all arms the same number of extra loops.

Uniformity

If sections become uneven, use extra loops to expand shorter sections. Check the uniformity of the wrappings as you work. Measure the wrappings on each arm periodically, and make small corrections as needed.

Color Changes

Start and end the same color on the same arm. After ending one color, move to a new arm to start another color. These procedures will keep color sections even all around. Start and end colors with a double half-hitch, and glue the ends in place. As you wrap, cover exposed yarn ends with new wrappings.

Ojo Variations

Form designs by changing yarn colors and wrapping methods. Each wrapping method produces a distinct look. Some methods demonstrated below are the back wrap, wing wrap, space wrap and star wrap.

6–16 Back wrap. Pass yarn under and over each arm. Creates recessed areas.

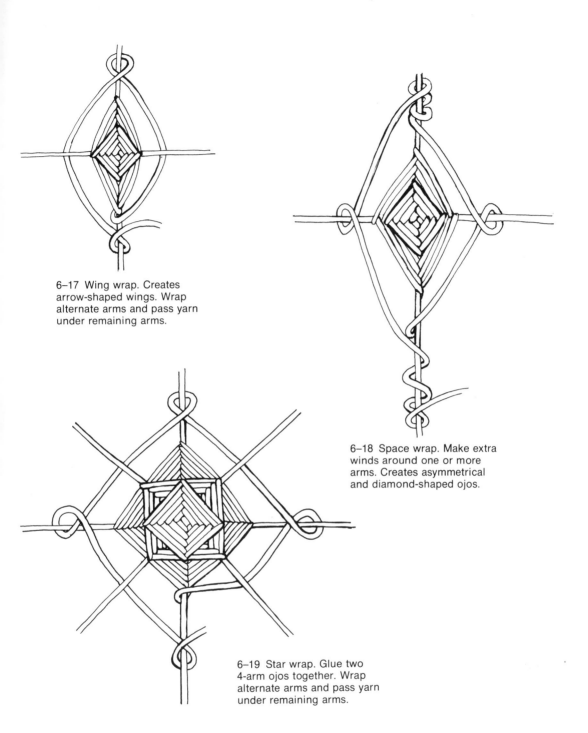

6–17 Wing wrap. Creates arrow-shaped wings. Wrap alternate arms and pass yarn under remaining arms.

6–18 Space wrap. Make extra winds around one or more arms. Creates asymmetrical and diamond-shaped ojos.

6–19 Star wrap. Glue two 4-arm ojos together. Wrap alternate arms and pass yarn under remaining arms.

Finishing the Ojo de Dios

Wrap dowel ends one at a time. Wind yarn onto each arm, ending with a double half-hitch. Glue the yarn end in place. If desired, wrap in a feather or two, or tie on tassels, pom-poms or fringes.

KNOTTING: ALL PLANT HANGERS ASIDE

Don't get me wrong. I called this chapter "All Plant Hangers
Aside," but I have nothing against plants or plant hangers. In
fact, I have them all over my apartment. I have simple hangers,
double hangers, hangers with tassels and wall pockets over-
flowing with greenery. For me and countless others, making a
new plant hanger is a joy. By now, however, almost every
crafter knows how to knot a plant hanger, belt or wall hanging.
If not, there are already enough books on the subject. That is
precisely why this chapter takes a different approach to knotting.

Knotting has many applications. That is one of the reasons
the craft is so popular. For another reason, the techniques are
simple to master. Everyone knows how to tie knots. It's part of
every mother's standard curriculum. However, when we strug-
gled through out first shoelace-tying lessons, we never sus-
pected those same skills would go into artwork. All we saw
then were tangled masses of shoelaces.

The art of knotting resurfaced in the 60s after many years of
neglect. At that time, crafters rediscovered the knotter's art
called *macrame,* and began knotting belts, purses, wall hangings and all kinds of home and fashion accessories. Not much
later, America also rediscovered the joy of houseplants. At
that time, the macrame fad grew to epidemic proportions.
Nearly everyone caught the fever.

For some people, houseplants became an all-consuming pas-
sion. Folks who never knew a philodendron from a eucalyptus
tree spent time talking to their greenery. There were plants ev-
erywhere. Macrame let people hang their plants up. Crafters
knotted hangers and more hangers. With macrame so appropriate for planters, aside from the craft's original appeal, knotting became by far the country's favorite craft by the mid-70s.

Today, there are many approaches to knotting. This chapter
includes many works that stray from the familiar macrame look.
At first glance, some seem more like weaving or coiling than
macrame. Others look like lacy, free-form spider webs. In fact,
this lacy knotting technique is often referred to as *needlelace.*

No matter what the techniques are called, however, knots are familiar to all of us. It is the application that changes. In this chapter, the traditional knots are all included. As you'll see, how you use them makes all the difference.

THE KNOTTING PROCESS

We all know how to tie knots. As a consequence, there isn't much to say about the knotting process. Knotting becomes a fibercraft when we tie knots into decorative patterns. The knotted works that result are as suited to grace a special wall as a painting, weaving or signed lithograph.

Most basic knots are familiar to us, whether we know it or not. If we didn't learn the square knot, half-hitch, overhand knot and lark's head knot by the time we graduated from the Brownies or Cub Scouts, then we probably learned them in another fibercraft. Many of the same, or nearly identical, knots have a purpose in weaving, crochet, stitchery and other crafts.

The half-hitch, for example, has relatives in almost every fibercraft. The names are different, but the knot is the same. Needlelace-knotting, which is based on the half-hitch, is increasing rapidly in popularity. In needlelace-knotting, half-hitches create a network of open, lacy designs reminiscent of a spider's web (Fig. 7–2). Later in this chapter, a needlelace circle is demonstrated step-by-step.

MATERIALS

It used to seem mandatory for knotting materials to be jute, sisal, wrapping twine, cable cord or synthetic versions of these cords. Indeed many artists still knot magnificent structures with nothing but the traditional cords. Today however, as the concept of knotting has expanded, the choice is much greater. The reason is not that the requirements for knotting cords have changed. Strength and very little stretch, the main characteristics of the traditional cords, are still essential. The reason so many new fibers appear in knotting is that fiberartists today are more experimental and less tied to tradition.

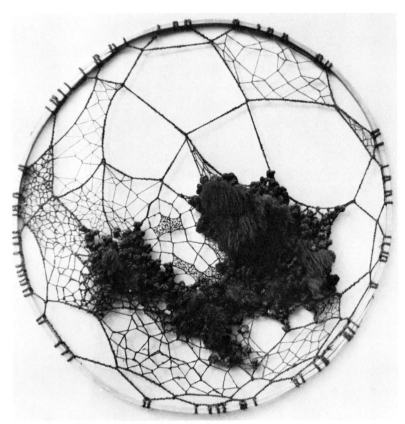

7–2 Needlelace circle. Robin Brisco. 31″ diameter. Novelty yarns and fake fur on a wooden circle. Photographed by Chet Brisco.

The examples in this chapter feature wools, novelty yarns, silk and fabric lengths among other fibers (Fig. 7–3). If you choose, mix fibers together. Mary Ann York's African basket in Figure 7–4, for example, mixes linen and German rug wool. Needlelace projects are perfect for fiber combinations. As you'll see from examples later in the chapter, the same needlelace project is likely to encompass soft wool, skinny linen and nubby novelty yarn.

In knotted projects, the amount of fiber is especially difficult to determine in advance. Except for open, lacy projects like needlelace, knotting as a rule uses what seems to be an extraordinary amount of cord. Thick cords get used up more quickly than thin cords. In addition, tight, close knots use more cord than loose, widely spaced knots. Experience will tell you how much cord you'll need. For the first few projects, start with cords that are several times longer than the finished length desired.

To keep tension in the cords, you'll also need something to

7–4 African basket. Mary Ann York. 9$^{1}/_{2}$″ x 10″. Double half-hitch in brown linen and beige German rug wool. Beads and feathers added. Photograph by Rich Tardif.

hold the cords. For small projects, the standard tools are T-pins and a macrame board. Special macrame boards are available at craft shops, but sections of cork, Styrofoam or Celotex board (available at building supply stores or lumberyards) work equally well. For large hanging pieces, suspend the cords from a nail in the wall, ceiling beam, drapery rod or any convenient place. Just be sure the chosen fixture is sturdy and high enough to let the cords hang down straight.

It is sometimes desirable to work inside a frame. The frame

127 KNOTTING

7–5 The Cow in the Middle. Libby Platus. 18′ x 8′ x 1¹/₂′. Double half-hitch in sisal. Worked from an armature at the top. Balance of sculpture is completely self-supported. Photograph courtesy of the artist.

7–6 Triptych. Center panel. Libby Platus. 4½' x 13' x 2'. Double half-hitch in sisal. Created in three separate panels for Blue Cross of Southern California in Woodland Hills, CA. Lemon yellow, gold, orange and red orange. Photograph by Barbara Probstein.

then becomes part of the finished piece. Many needlelace projects, for example, take this approach. For the frame, use any rigid object, like a wooden circle, wheel rim, bent wire or driftwood.

To make a needlelace project like the one in Figure 7–16 choose three different yarns in varying weights and textures, a wooden circle, scissors and a yarn needle. The yarns shown are Lily Mills Sheeps Coat, pearl cotton and cotton lace yarn.

COLOR AND FORM

For years, knotted pieces seemed to take shape in natural and neutral colors only. There were practical reasons at first. Originally nothing but natural colors were available in the traditional macrame fibers. Artists who preferred color had to dye their own fibers. Today, however, almost all fibers come in a huge variety of colors. Jute and sisal, the stars of the knotter's art, as well as wools, cottons and nearly every other fiber are now available in neutrals, pastels and brilliant, eye-popping colors. Still, for some artists, form is what really counts and color is secondary.

"Color helps to define the shape, and add rhythm and richness," states Libby Platus, whose knotted sculptures appear in architectural settings throughout the country. It is the structure

7–7 Snow on a Pine Bough. Kathrine Browne. 33″ x 39″. Free-form knotting based on double half-hitch and lark's head knots. Wools, cottons and synthetics. Photograph courtesy of the artist.

and texture that is most important to Ms. Platus. "I work in shapes," she adds. "If I do a piece without color, I'm just as happy."

Libby Platus creates free-form fiberworks in double half hitches. Through cross-tension knotting techniques, large sculptures maintain their shapes even in antigravity positions, according to the artist. "The Cow in the Middle," for example, in Figure 7–5 has an armature at the top only. Other pieces by Ms. Platus have no armature at all.

The sculptural potential of knotting is indeed exciting. In addition, knotting lends to solid, two-dimensional pieces and openwork designs. All forms are included in this chapter. As

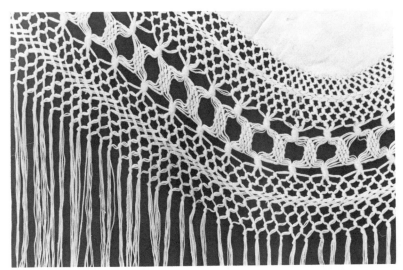

7–8 Knotted fringe. Silk fringe from an antique shawl. Almost entirely overhand knots.

you will see, many different effects are possible by using the same simple knots in different ways.

THE KNOTS

Basic knots and variations appear in Figures 7–10 to 7–14. Many knots require two kinds of cords: the *knotting* cords and the *anchor* cords. Knotting cords tie over anchor cords. Anchor cords are merely a foundation for the knots. As a consequence, it is possible to substitute any other foundation for the anchor cords. Work the knotting cords the same way, whether you are tying them over anchor cords, dowels, driftwood, circles, armatures or whatever your project calls for.

Reverse Lark's Head

The basic starting knot is the reverse lark's head knot (Fig. 7–10). Fold one cord in half. Loop the folded end over the

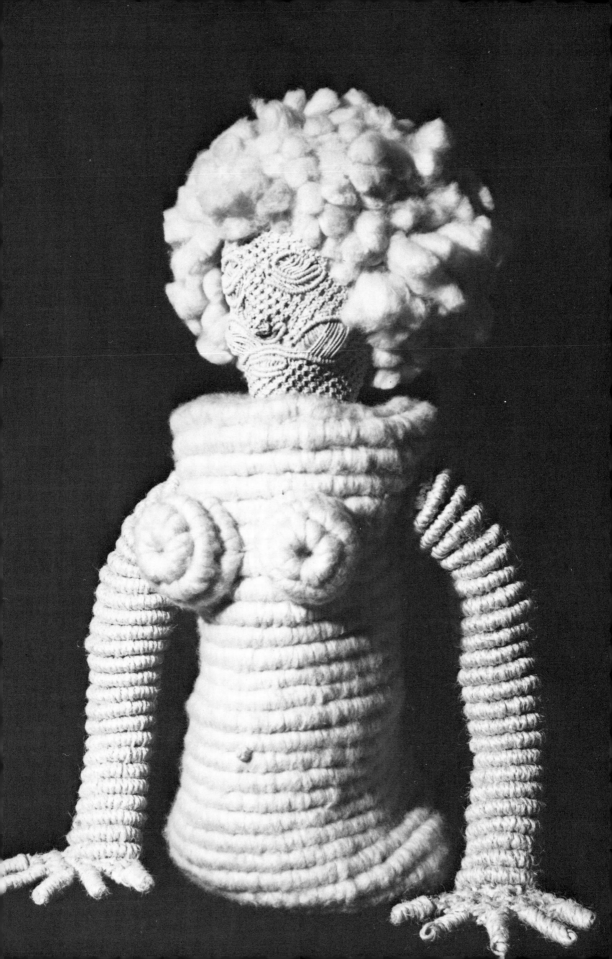

7–9 (*Opposite page*) Matilda. Sharon La Pierre. 36″ high. Macrame sculpture with predominantly square-knotted face and hitched body. White wool and sisal. Photograph by Phil Kepner.

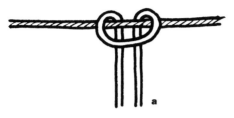

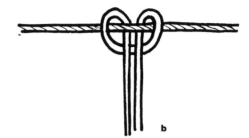

7–10 Starting knot known as reverse lark's head knot.

anchor cord (Fig. 7–10a). Pull the ends through the loop (Fig. 7–10b).

The reverse lark's head knot is a typical starting knot. It holds all cords on a horizontal anchor cord or any other foundation. Tie it over an anchor cord, circle, armature, driftwood, frame or anyplace else you wish to start a new cord.

Overhand Knot

To work an overhand knot, loop the end of the cord up and under itself (Fig. 7–11a). Bring the end through the loop (Fig. 7–11b). Pull to tighten.

The overhand knot is probably one of the first knots you learned to tie. We use it without thinking for tying packages or securing clotheslines. In the fibercrafts, it is the most convenient knot for tying fiber ends that might otherwise fray. If you look at the antique fringe in Figure 7–8, you'll see the knot's decorative potential.

7–11 Overhand knot.

133 KNOTTING

Square Knot

To work a square knot, bring the right cord over the center cords and under the left cord (Fig. 7–12a). Bring the left cord under the center cords and over the right cord. Pull outside cords (Fig. 7–12b). Bring the left cord over the center cords and under the right cord (Fig. 7–12c). Bring the right cord under the center cords and over the left cord. Pull outside cords to tighten the knot (Fig. 7–12d).

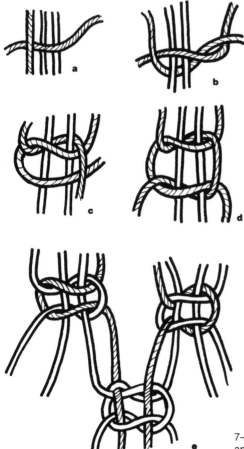

7–12 Square knot (a–d) and alternating square knot (e).

Alternating Square Knot

To make an alternating square knot, complete one row of square knots as usual. In the next row, use the right cords of one group and the left cords of the neighboring group to make the new knots (Fig. 7–12e).

For an open network of knots, use the alternating square knot. You can see the alternating square knot in the face of Sharon La Pierre's "Matilda" in Figure 7–9.

Double Half-Hitch

To work a double half-hitch, bring an anchor cord across the other cords (Fig. 7–13a). Loop the neighboring cord over the anchor cord and under to the left (Fig. 7–13b). Bring the same cord back over the anchor cord to the right of the loop you have created. Then loop it under the anchor cord to the left of the new loop that you are creating (Fig. 7–13c).

When the anchor cord is brought back and forth across the knotting cords as in Figure 7–13d, the result is a solid knotted section that looks very much like coiling.

The double half-hitch in Figures 7–13a to 7–13c are tied left to right. Although the knotting principles do not change, sometimes it is easier to tie the knots from right to left. Figures 7–13e and 7–13f show the double half-hitch tied right to left.

If your knotting cord comes from beneath the anchor cord or foundation, the appearance again differs slightly. This occurs, for example, when you warp a hoop for a circle weaving project. This version of the double half-hitch appears in Figure 7–13g.

The double half-hitch is extremely important in the knotter's art. Depending upon how the knots are tied, the double half-hitch creates an open pattern, or solid knotted sections of sculptural pieces. The double half-hitch is also used in countless other fibercrafts from weaving to ojo-making. Sometimes it is called the clove hitch.

Half-Hitch

The half-hitch is shown in Figure 7–14. It is so simple, it hardly needs an explanation. For each half-hitch, loop the

7-13 Double half-hitch
tied left to right (a–c) and
right to left (e and f);
(d) shows result of knotted
section; (g) shows another
version.

knotting cord over the anchor cord. If your knotting cord is
traveling to the right, loop the cord on the left side (Fig. 7–14a).
If your knotting cord is traveling to the left, loop the cord on
the right side (Fig. 7–14b).

To make rows of half-hitch knots, start each row with two
half-hitches that are close together. In other words, start with a

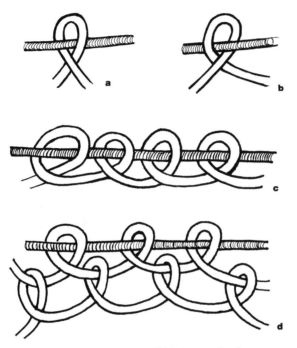

7–14 Half-hitch (a, b) and half-hitch rows (c, d).

double half-hitch. The double half-hitch will keep the starting knot in place. A row of half-hitches appears in Figure 7–14c. Tie rows of half-hitches by using the upper cords as anchor cords for the new row (Fig. 7–14d).

Half-hitch rows are sometimes called knotless netting. However, whether you call the rows *knotted* or *knotless,* it is the same half-hitch, and very easy to do.

MAKING A NEEDLELACE CIRCLE

Figures 7–15 and 7–16 show examples of needlelace circles. Figure 7–17a–e shows how to make a needlelace circle. The needlelace technique demonstrated here uses nothing but half-hitches and double half-hitches. The technique is easy and extremely enjoyable. Compared to the intricate lace masterworks

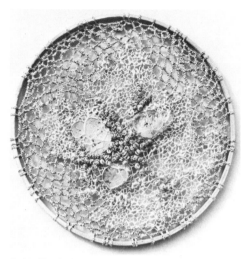

7–15 Needlelace circle. Robin Brisco. 9″
diameter. An intricate network of novelty yarns.
French knots dot the center section. Sea glass
is caught in the yarn network. Browns.
Photograph by Chet Brisco.

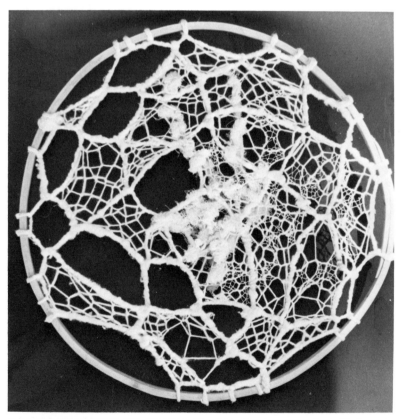

7–16 Needlelace circle. 24″ diameter. All white. Handspun wool, unplied wool,
and cotton boucle.

from centuries ago, this version has a far more random and open look. The new technique is related to traditional needle-work nonetheless. It is very simplified, however, and many purists would probably describe it as a distant cousin.

Making a Yarn Framework

To make a yarn framework, tie a double half-hitch to a wooden circle. Half-hitch around the circle at random intervals (Fig. 7–17a). Pull the yarn taut after each knot to secure knot to circle. (The circle used in Figures 7–17a to e is 8½ inches in diameter. Yarns are Lily Mills Sheepcoat, perle cotton and cotton lace.).

Make the framework a bulky fiber or smooth yarn. Save especially interesting textures and skinniest yarns for filling in the framework. Either use a yarn needle with about 3 feet of yarn, or use a center-pull ball as shown in Figure 4–5.

Hitch the next row to the previous row of yarn (Fig. 7–17b). Keep half-hitching until you reach the center of the circle.

Complete the yarn framework with a double half-hitch at the center. Trim the end to 1 inch. You will now have a framework composed of shapes outlined in yarn.

7–17a Making a yarn framework.

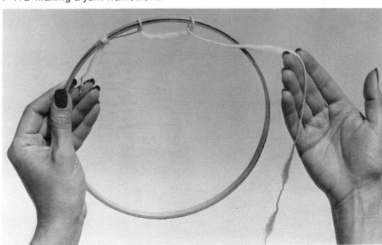

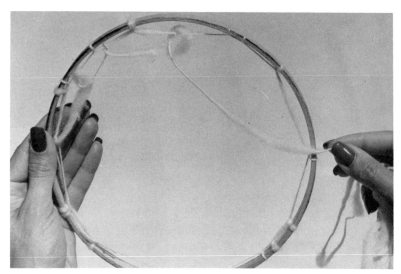

7–17b Hitch to the previous row of yarn. Keep half-hitching until you reach the center of the circle.

7–17c Fill in as many outlined shapes as desired.

Filling in Shapes

To fill in the shapes, choose one of the areas outlined in yarn to start (Fig. 7–17c). Just as you made the yarn framework inside the circle, half-hitch a new network inside the yarn shape. You'll probably find it easiest to use your needle to fill the inside areas. When you reach the center of a shape, double half-hitch across yarns until you reach the next shape. Fill in as many shapes as desired.

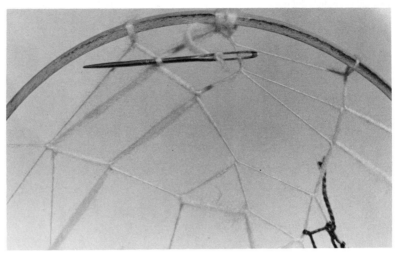

7-17d Stitch ends through the nearest half-hitch.

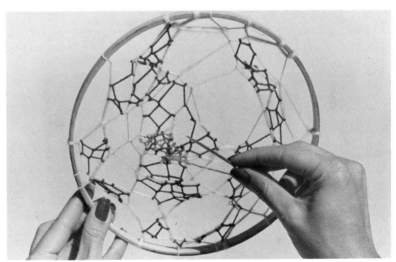

7-17e Fill in as much or as little of the circle as desired.

Finishing the Circle

To hide ends, thread them on the yarn needle and stitch through the nearest half-hitch (Fig. 7–17d).

To finish the circle, use the thinnest yarn and half-hitch a new network of yarns on the other yarns. Fill in as much or as little of the circle as desired (Fig. 7–17e).

The new needlelace exhibits a freedom that appeals to modern fiberartists. The craft is also interesting because almost anything provides a frame for the knotted networks. As you'll see in Figures 7–18 to 7–21, circles, boxes, bent wire and a room divider frame all make interesting settings for needlelace.

7-18 Needlelace Web. Robin Brisco. 24″ x 24″. Needlelace knotting in a wooden nursery flat. Wool and angora structure. Mexican handspun details. Bark added. Black and browns. Photograph by Chet Brisco.

7-19 Apparent Apathy. B. J. Adams. 12″ x 11″ x 11″. Stuffed sculpture surrounded by a needlelace network. Wood base. Nylon upholstery thread. Velvet, satin, wool and synthetic fabrics. Photograph courtesy of the artist.

7-20 (*Opposite page*) Room divider mock-up. Barbara Smith. 12″ x 8″ model for 5′ x 3′ room divider. Conso cord needlelace sections. Wool wrapped over jute. Photograph by Mel Smith.

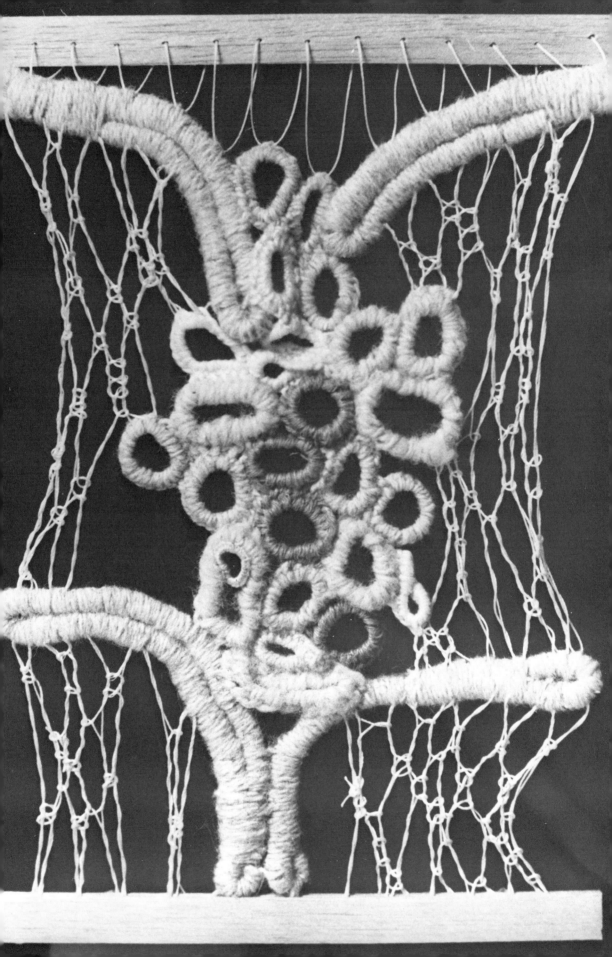

7–21 Needlelace necklace. Robin Brisco. 7″ x 8″ pendant. Needlelace network of novelty yarns, framed in wrapped copper wire. Ivory and brown tones. Photograph by Chet Brisco.

NON-LOOM WEAVING: CIRCLES & OTHER NON-LOOMS

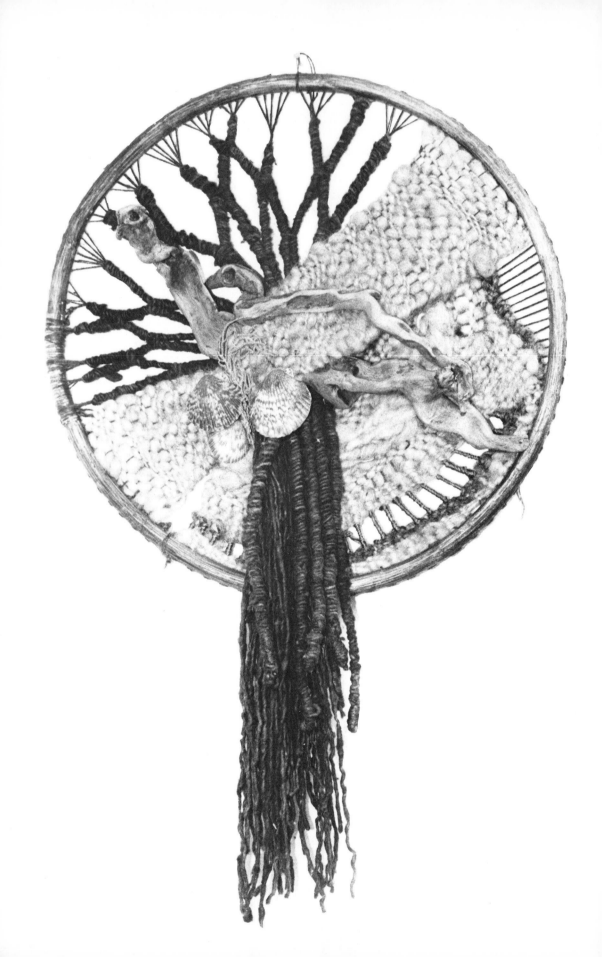

There's so much to say about weaving. Volumes and volumes overflow from library shelves on this fibercraft alone. Even if I knew all there is to know about weaving, I couldn't fit all the information into one book—let alone one chapter. So here's one aspect of weaving. That aspect is non-loom weaving, on circles and other rigid frames. Non-loom weaving appeals to beginners and experienced weavers alike. No special equipment is required. Your frame, which can be nearly anything, remains part of the finished artwork.

Non-loom weaving is increasingly popular, especially in circle frames. As you'll see from the weavings in this chapter, "the bigger the better" is the rule. Take a look at Rozann Johnson's spectacular, multitextured works in Figure 8–1 and on the front cover. Most of her pieces are at least a few feet in diameter. Her weaving on the cover, in fact, was the smallest available for the photo session. That one is nearly 4 feet around.

Personally, I like to work big. For one thing, there's lots of room to experiment in a big circle. For another thing, little mistakes stay hidden (where they belong). My first circle was a big one. I started it at the Rusty Needle in Laguna Beach, California. The Rusty Needle is a fabulous shop, set in an old Spanish home overlooking the Pacific. Besides stocking every kind of yarn imaginable, the shop holds workshops where fiberartists can get together to exchange ideas and learn new techniques.

At my first circle weaving workshop, I chose a 4-foot hoop and yarns. When I picked out the supplies, I knew the circle would be beautiful on a large, then-empty wall. So I warped the loom, and wove my way to closing time. So far, so good—until I brought the circle to my car. Unfortunately, I had a mini-Honda then. At one time, when I lived in New York, the car was wonderful for parking on New York City streets. That day, it seemed terrible for an ambitious circle weaver with a long drive home up the California coast. There it was, all spelled out in my mind—that "plan ahead" sign with the "d" falling off the plaque.

No matter how I turned the weaving, it wouldn't fit into the car. Not the door, trunk or window. Not even if I let the stick shift poke through the warp yarns. There was only one

8–1 Hoop tapestry. Rozann Johnson. 8′ x 4$\frac{1}{2}$′ Plain weave with long lengths of hanging fibers. Wool, jute and synthetics. Blue and beige.

8-2 Vesta. Claudia Cornwell Wilbourn. 41″ x 36″. Sculptural weaving on steel armature and base of Manzanita burl. Warped and wrapped in goat hair. Handspun wool in earth tones, orange, rose, red and blue. Armature welded by Ms. Wilbourn and Kurt Shull. Photograph by John Grady.

solution—a good friend with a bigger car, to pick up the circle the next day.

If there is a moral to the story, it's not to keep your weaving small. The message is that weaving is an adventure.

ABOUT NON-LOOM WEAVING AND THE WEAVING PROCESS

There is much talk these days about non-loom weaving and whether it exists at all. Many weavers, probably some who are reading these words, will tell you that there's no such thing as non-loom weaving. Anything that holds warp yarns, they'll say, is a loom. While there is truth in that philosophy, *non-loom* weaving is still the best description I've found for weaving with-

8–3 Lampshade. Mary Ellen Cannon. 14″ high. Frame is wrapped in chenille, warped in nylon, woven in Irish looped yarn. Predominantly white, with gold, grey and brown tones. Photograph courtesy of the artist.

out traditional looms. Non-loom weaving, as described in this chapter, means weaving without a floor loom, table-top loom, inkle loom, backstrap loom, frame loom, cardboard loom or anything else that is specially invented for weaving and detached after the piece is woven.

Every weaving example in this chapter requires no more equipment than you see in the photographs. Whatever acts as the loom is incorporated in the work. Most non-loom weaving is done with a yarn needle or your fingers. You can incorporate

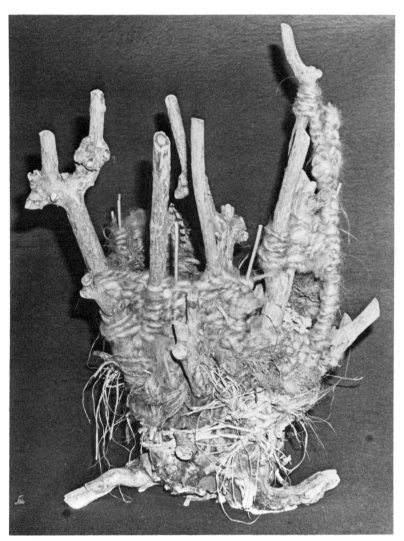

8–4 Root basket. Nan Hackett Joe. 24″ high. Protruding roots turn into the warp for a twined basket. Handspun wool.

a variety of weaves and other fiber techniques such as wrapping, knotting and collage.

Weaving itself is easy to learn. The weaver works with two yarns—the *warp* and the *weft*. Warp threads stretch across the loom, most often in vertical parallel lines. The weft yarns pass under and over the warp threads. If you learned weaving at all as a child, you probably learned to weave in neat, straight lines. In today's non-loom weaving, as you'll see in this chapter, you don't have to weave in straight lines, or even warp in straight lines. Non-loom weaving is a wonderful place to experiment.

MATERIALS

The non-loom and yarns are your basic materials. The non-loom is any sturdy frame to hold the warp yarns. Some suggestions are wooden circles, metal macrame hoops, hula hoops, bamboo and barrel hoops, lamp frames, metal armatures, wheel rims, curving driftwood, tree roots and canvas stretchers. The frame must be rigid all around. Circles, the most popular frames, are available in a range of sizes at most weaving and craft shops.

If you choose a metal or plastic frame, you'll also need a roll of masking tape. The masking tape covers the frame and helps keep the wrappings from slipping.

Weaving requires several kinds of yarns. If you want to cover the hoop, you'll need a coarse, heavy or highly textured fiber for wrapping. Avoid slippery yarns. Just as masking tape holds the wrappings better than metal or plastic, the wrappings hold the warp yarns better than plain frames. Berber yarn and commercial handspuns are good choices. Select a neutral color or something to harmonize with your weaving shades.

For the warp, choose a strong fiber with very little stretch. Test yarns for strength by pulling a length in your hands. If it breaks, don't consider it. Traditionally, warp yarns are thin and neutral-colored. The reason for a neutral warp is that weft yarns are the major design element in most weavings. As a general rule, therefore, stay away from heavy yarns or bright colors. Use dark or light warp threads. A dark warp gives a richer effect. As a result, many weavers always use deep brown or black. A few good choices are linen, goat hair and cotton carpet warp. As long as they're strong and sturdy, however, other cottons, wools and synthetics are also appropriate.

8–5 Circle weaving. 18″ diameter. Dark goat hair warp remains visible through white handspun wool, and hidden behind darker, tightly beaten wool yarns. Metal macrame frame. Plain weave with soumak. Circle originally appeared in *Creative Crafts Magazine,* Newton, N.J.

For the weft, there are no rules at all. Consider anything in any texture and weight. Don't be limited by yarns alone, even though the choice is considerable. Natural grasses, twigs, leather or almost anything works as weft. The more interesting the fibers, the better. Mix fibers of different textures, weights and colors. If you are working on a first project, heavy yarns are highly recommended. Heavy yarn cuts down the working time considerably. The heavier the yarn, the fewer rows you are going to weave. Some wonderful heavy fibers are roving, hand-

153 NON-LOOM WEAVING

spun wools and "thick and thin" yarns. Heavy yarns lend to bold abstracts. Thin yarns, on the other hand, are better for pictures, details and intricate designs.

No matter what yarns you choose, you'll also need a blunt yarn needle, scissors and beater. Special beaters, which push the weft yarns closer together, are available at craft or fiber shops. Wide-toothed combs, "afro" combs and forks, however, are adequate substitutes for commercial beaters.

WEAVING A CIRCLE

Figures 8–6a to d give guidelines for weaving a circle like the one in Figure 8–5. If you prefer another shape frame, follow the basic steps anyway. The same principles apply to almost all types of non-looms.

Wrapping the Circle

Wrapping the hoop is partly for decoration and partly for keeping the warp yarns from sliding around the hoop. If the frame is coarse or uneven enough to keep warp yarns secure, wrapping becomes a matter of choice. Driftwood, for example, is usually left unwrapped. Most pieces have nubs and nodules that catch the yarns and are too attractive to hide.

If the frame is slippery, wrap masking tape all around the frame before you cover it with yarns. For all metal or plastic hoops, masking tape is necessary. Wind the tape, sticky side down, all around the hoop. When wrapped, your masking tape surface will hold yarns better than the original slippery plastic or metal.

To wrap the circle, roll your yarn into a center-pull ball as shown in Figure 4–5. Lay the yarn end against the circle. Wind the ball of yarn over the end and around the circle (Fig. 8–6a).

Wind the yarn all around the circle. Wind it tight enough to cover the original wood, plastic, metal or other material in the frame. When you get back to your starting point, stitch the end through the first few winds (Fig. 8–6b).

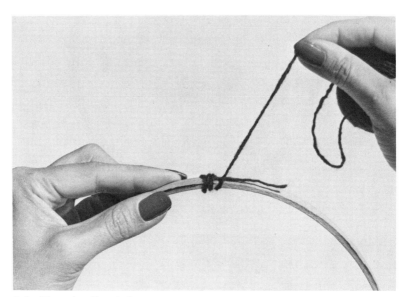

8–6a Wrapping the circle.

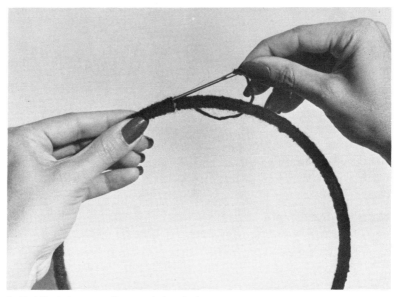

8–6b Wind the yarn all around the circle.

8–6c Warping the circle.

8–6d Alternately tie the warp threads to the top and bottom of the circle until you reach the side edge.

Warping the Circle

Dressing or *warping* the loom is usually the first step in weaving. This means tying the warp yarns to the loom. Figures 8–6a to d show one warping method—a full frame with vertical warp. Whether you use this method or another, the spacing of the warp threads determines how tight or how loose the weave will be. Warp threads that are close together result in a tight weave. Warp threads that are further apart create a loose weave. Also, as a general rule, the closer the warp threads, the more visible they will be in the finished weaving.

To warp the circle as in Figure 8–6c, use the double half-hitch to tie the warp yarn to center top and bottom of the circle. Keep the warp yarn taut, but not so tight that it distorts the circle. If your circle is especially large or unstable, tie a rope across the width to counterbalance the pull of the warp threads.

Working from the center, alternately tie the warp threads to the top and bottom of the circle until you reach one side edge. Then warp the other side of the circle. Space warp threads close together or far apart, depending upon how tight a weave you desire. The circle above has four warp threads to the inch. Stitch loose ends through the wrappings on the frame.

Securing the Warp with a Chain Stitch

At the perimeter of the circle, chain stitch around the warp threads. The chain stitch further helps to keep warp threads in place. In addition, the stitching creates better separation and more even spacing of the warp yarns. The chain stitch is shown in Figure 8–7.

To work the chain stitch, tie a knot on the first warp. Stitch under the next warp with yarn looped under the needle (Fig. 8–7a). When you pull the needle, the result is a loop around the yarn. For all remaining stitches, stitch through the previous loop. Then stitch under the next warp with yarn looped under the needle as before (Fig. 8–7b).

8–7 Chain stitch.

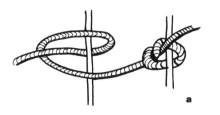
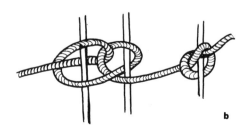

a   b

8–8 Circle weaving. Jerry Forburger. Circular warp on 14″ rings. At left, Mountain Sheep. Work in progress at right, The Eagle. Both in wool yarns. Photograph courtesy of the artist.

ALTERNATE WARP METHODS

There are many ways to warp circles or other non-looms. Instead of the full-frame, vertical warp as in the example in Figure 8–6, some artists prefer partial warps or circular warps.

For a circular warp, take a look at Figure 8–8. In the photo, Jerry Forburger shows a completed circle and a weaving in progress. Both feature circular warps. As you can see, the artist attaches her warp yarns using a different method from the one demonstrated here. However, the circular pattern of the warp is clear to see.

To make this circular warp, draw the first thread from the top to bottom of the hoop as usual. Bring the next thread to the top of the hoop, and tie it to the left of the last warp thread. Bring the next thread to the bottom of the hoop, and tie it to the right of the last warp thread. Repeat this process until the circle is all filled in.

Take a look through the photographs in this chapter. You will see that warping methods vary greatly from weaving to weaving. As in all phases of non-loom weaving, feel free to experiment.

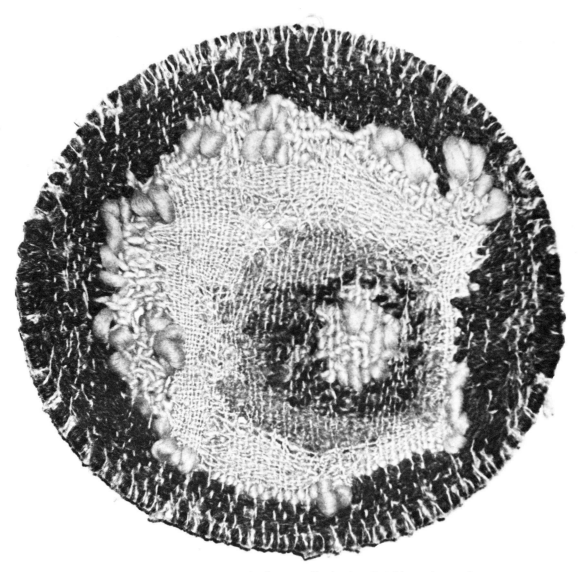

8–9 Circle weaving. 12″ diameter. Predominantly tabby and soumak weaves. Note leno sections in palest area. Yellow to dark brown wools. Metal macrame hoop. Circle originally appeared in *Creative Crafts Magazine,* Newton, NJ.

159 NON-LOOM WEAVING

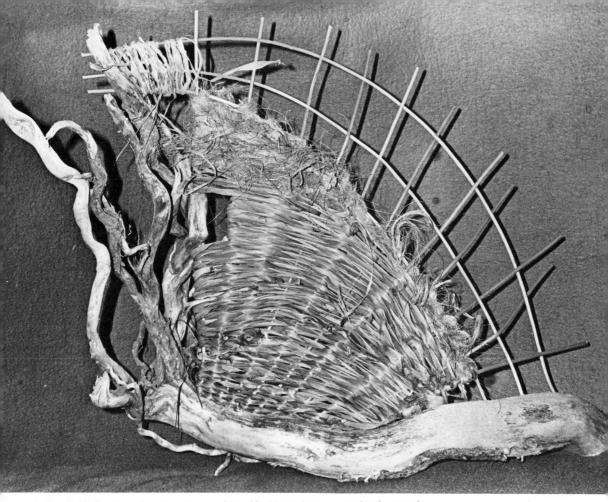

8–10 Twining. Nan Hackett Joe. 23″ x 26″. Natural grasses twined around a reed warp. Gnarled driftwood frame.

WEAVING METHODS

Your yarns and how you weave them determine the design and texture of the piece (Figs. 8–9 and 8–10). Different weaves are illustrated in Figures 8–11 to 8–15. Each has its own special characteristics. The plain weave is the most basic. Some weavers use nothing else. Other weavers add textural variations. Try one or several weaves. You'll find they all have interesting possibilities.

Tabby or Plain Weave

Figure 8–11 shows the tabby or plain weave. Weave the weft yarns under and over the warp threads. Reverse direction and weave back again. Be sure to weave under the warp threads passed over in the last row. This is the most basic weave. To vary the weave, skip over or under more than one warp thread at a time.

Soumak

Figure 8–12 shows soumak weave. Loop the yarn over two warp threads and back under one. Depending upon how tight the loops are, the result is a loopy look or a wrapped-warp look. To vary the weave, leave large and small loops, or loop the yarn over more than two warp threads at a time. For loops that move in the same direction, alternate with rows of the plain weave.

Leno

Figure 8–13 shows leno weave. Using any two warp threads, pull the second warp thread over the first warp thread. Bring the weft over the first new warp thread, and under the new second warp thread. Repeat with each pair of warp threads in the row. In the next row, keep warp threads in their original sequence. Weave under and over the warp threads in the row using a plain weave.

The result is an open weave. Since the warp threads twist in the leno weave, they tend to tighten. It is necessary therefore to have a resilient warp for this weave.

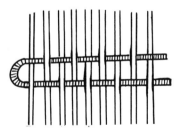

8–11 Tabby or plain weave.

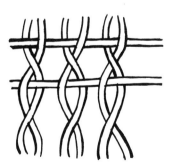

8–12 Soumak.

8–13 Leno.

Ghiordes Knot

Figure 8–14 shows the Ghiordes knot. On each pair of warp threads, loop the weft yarn under the warp to the right, over both warp threads, and back under the left warp thread. Use separate lengths for long fringes (Fig. 8–14a). Use a continuous weft for loops or pile (Fig. 8–14b). For pile, cut the loops when the rows are completed. Be sure to alternate each knotted row with two or more rows of plain weave. The Ghiordes knot results in looping sections, rug-like pile or long hanging lengths.

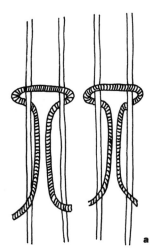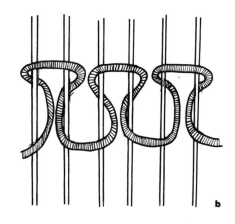

8–14 Ghiordes knot.

Twining

Figure 8–15 shows twining. Knot two weft yarns together. Hold one yarn in back of the warp threads, and the other yarn in front. Cross weft yarns between the warp threads for a *half* turn (Fig. 8–15a), or twist the yarns between the warp threads for a *full* turn (Fig. 8–15b).

Use weft yarns in the same or different colors. With different colors, the half-turn lets colors alternate on warp threads. The full-turn leaves a dot of the alternate color between warp threads.

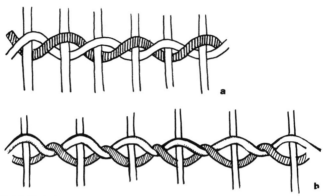

8–15 Twining.

WEAVING THE DESIGN

Weave thin or medium-weight yarns with a blunt yarn needle. Weave heavy yarns with your fingers.

Figure 8–16 demonstrates one easy way to create a design in yarns. Using the plain weave, "draw" outlines for your design with your yarn needle. Let the yarn wander freely. Push yarn to

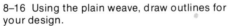

8–16 Using the plain weave, draw outlines for your design.

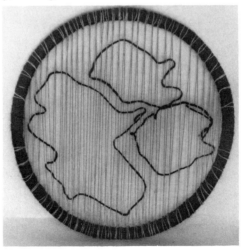

change shapes, or keep weaving until you are satisfied with the design (Fig. 8–16).

Weave in the design areas. Weave in an arc, and push the arc close to the last row with your beater. This process is called *bubbling* the yarn and *beating* it in (Fig. 8–17).

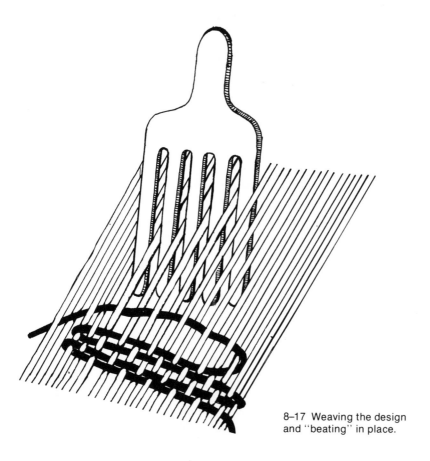

8–17 Weaving the design and "beating" in place.

Weave with a comfortable length of yarn. Try a 2-yard length at first. If you prefer a longer or shorter length, cut your next weft yarn accordingly. Take care, however, to keep yarns that tend to fray in short lengths. By the time they pass through warp thread after warp thread, soft yarns often look shaggy or worn out.

8–18 Tower of David. Marianne Mencher. 16″ x
13″. Wire frame, with sections outlined in wire
and monofilament line. Interlocking yarns
provide transitions between color sections.
Wool and wool blends. Photograph courtesy of
the artist.

Hide ends in the nearest row. As you start new lengths of
yarn, leave a few inches hanging out of the weaving. Later, tuck
the end into the weave.

Be sure your weave is not too tight and not too loose. If the
weave is too tight, the warp threads pull together. If the weave
is too loose, the overall effect is somewhat messy. The bubbling process keeps the weave from becoming too tight. In
beating, the arc flattens into a relaxed line. If you wish the warp
threads to show, leave the weft fairly loose. If you prefer to hide
the warp, however, beat the weft tight.

It is unnecessary, and to many artists undesirable, to weave
an entire piece in straight rows. By the same token, you are not

required to fill in the entire circle. Open spaces or uneven weaves characterize the majority of today's non-loom weaving.

Weave design areas in any order you like. Some weavers begin with the largest areas. Others work from the center to the outer edges. For smooth transitions between woven areas, use the dovetail, interlocking or slit tapestry technique. These techniques are shown in Figures 8–19 to 8–21.

Slit Tapestry Technique

To use the slit tapestry technique, weave as far as the last available warp thread in the area you are filling. Reverse direction and weave back again. The slit tapestry technique leaves slim, open outlines between design sections (Fig. 8–19).

8–19 Slit tapestry technique.

Dovetail Technique

For the dovetail technique, weave over the first warp thread in the adjacent section. Reverse direction and weave back again. This technique joins the design sections without leaving open space (Fig. 8–20).

Interlocking Technique

For the interlocking technique, weave through the looped end of the adjacent weft. Reverse direction and weave back again. Like the dovetail technique, the interlocking method leaves no open space (Fig. 8–21).

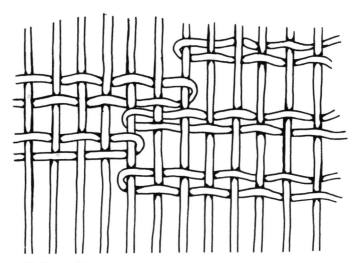

8–20 Dovetail technique.

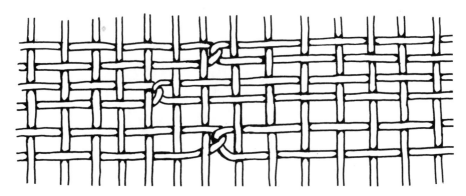

8–21 Interlocking technique.

PICTURES AND SCULPTURES

Some weavers paint pictures in yarns. Nan Hackett Joe, for example, has a face woven into her sunny hanging shown in the color section. Claudia Wilbourn takes another approach to representational weaving. She weaves sculptural creations on three-dimensional armatures. Her dramatic sculptures are shown in Figures 8–2 and 8–22.

For most pictures, the plain weave is best. To give you an idea of the wonderful pictures that are possible, two of Sharon La Pierre's tapestry people are shown in Figure 8–23. Although woven on more traditional looms, both faces are plain weaves that can be done on circles.

8–22 Strabo. Claudia Cornwell Wilbourn. 18″ high. Sculptural weaving on steel armature.
Wrapped and warped in goat hair. Brown, rose and black wools. On a wood base. Armature welded
by Ms. Wilbourn and Kurt Shull. Photograph by John Grady.

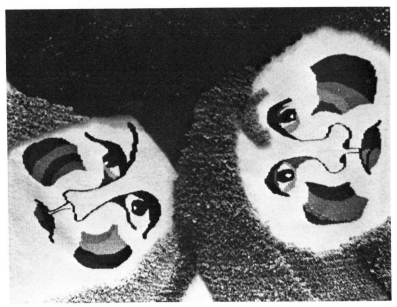

8–23 In Deepest Love and Memory of. . . . Sharon La Pierre. 3' x 5' Tabby weave, Ghiordes knots. Wool. Photograph by Pat Glover.

ENDINGS

It is never too late to add embellishments to your weaving. If you wish a fringe, tie on cords with the reverse lark's head knot. If you wish to add beads, buttons or bells, follow Figure 8–24. Following a line of weft, thread a bell, bead or button on the needle each time it surfaces in front of the weaving.

There is no end to how you can embellish your weaving. Add feathers, driftwood, seashells or wrapped cords (Fig. 8–25). As you've seen by now, non-loom weaving is a place for experimentation. Consider it a celebration of weaving, and let your imagination take over.

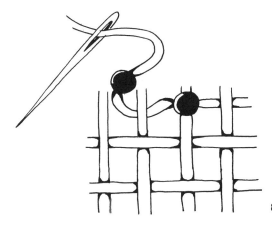

8–24 Adding embellishments.

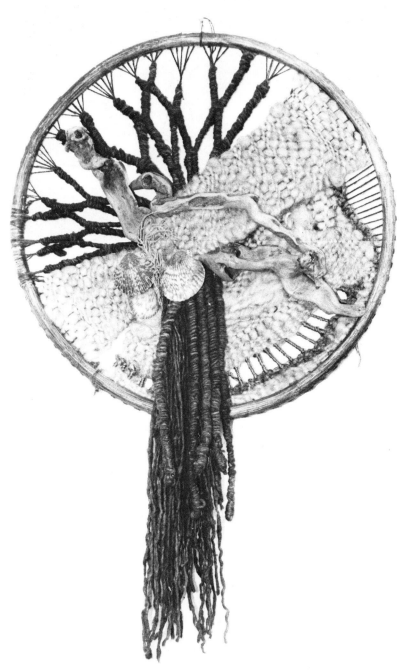

8–25 Circle weaving. Molly Hutchinson. 24″ diameter. Tabby weave and wrapped cords in a wooden circle. Embellished with driftwood, seashells and long hanging wrapped and unwrapped cords. Instead of warp yarns that tie onto the hoop, warp yarns pass through holes that have been drilled in the hoop. Photograph courtesy of the artist.

AND WHAT'S MORE

9–1 (*Opposite page*) Forest. Debbe Moss. 10' x 10' x 10'. Crocheted fibers include sisal, jute and manila hemp. Weighs 600 pounds total. Hand-dyed. Photograph by Hella Hammid.

Way back in Chapter 1, I said this book presents the entire spectrum of the fibercrafts. Truthfully, however, there are no limits to the medium. This book contains the most popular fibercrafts, but there are still many more. Some require special equipment, and others require different techniques. In addition, mixing and matching techniques is an art in itself.

Fibers lend themselves to so many techniques, whether you use the methods one at a time or all in the same piece. Sometimes, mixing techniques is unplanned as you find yourself changing techniques as you work. Sometimes your concepts change as the forms develop. The more fibercrafts you know, the more skills you have to draw on.

Debbe Moss is one artist who works with many different fiber techniques. Some pieces, like the KCET TV set in Figure 7–3, are massive. This particular fiberwork completely covers the sound apparatus on the television stage and incorporates weaving, knotting, crochet and tying. Her piece in Figure 9–1 is 10' x 10' x 10' and weighs 600 pounds!

At times the artist's concept evolves as she works. The Menage in Figure 9–2, for example, began as an idea for a fantasy dining environment, with crocheted metal tree forms and fiber-covered chairs. Instead, the Menage became the undulating crocheted dome you see here. "The work comes along and has its own life," according to Debbe Moss. "You have pre-conceived notions that evolve into something else. You have to let them happen."

If there is one concept that permeates the fibercrafts today, it is "let things happen." Experiment with different techniques, follow your feelings and let yourself go. Just as this book is a sampler of the fibercrafts, this chapter samples other techniques and combinations of techniques described in previous chapters. Perhaps you'll find new ways to combine the fibercrafts yourself. When you see the crocheted works and woven forms, you may even wish to sample other fibercrafts as well.

173 AND WHAT'S MORE

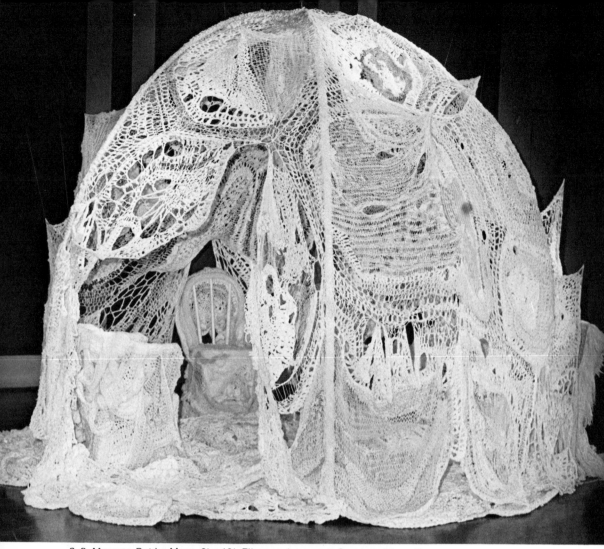

9–2 Menage. Debbe Moss. 8′ x 10′. Fiber environment. Crocheted in cotton, wool, satin nylon and assorted synthetics. Photograph by Nina Zacuto.

9–3 Grey Chip. Tom Fender. 17″ x 22″ x 2½″. Wrapped wool elements form a network over handmade paper. Photograph courtesy of the artist.

9–4 Valentine Pillow. Nan Hackett Joe. Woven on a frame loom, with stuffed and beaded hearts suspended from braided yarns. Multiple textures of red.

9–5 Doll basket. Sharon La Pierre. 25″ high. Figure 8 coiling, crocheted hair, tapestry face. All wool on a gourd base.

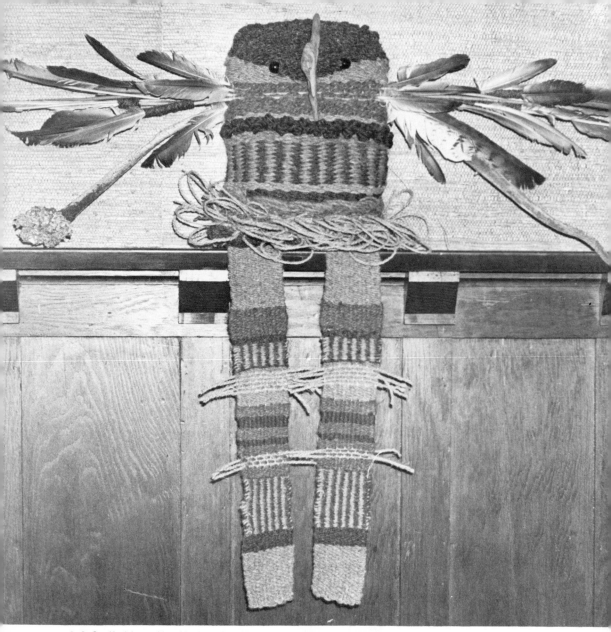

9–6 Stuffed form. Nan Hackett Joe. Woven owl, executed mainly in wools.
Stuffed body. Feather, driftwood and bead details.

Fiber Sources

The following list contains mail-order fiber sources and large fiber manufacturers. To see various yarns close up, the best idea is to visit a specialized shop. If you find difficulty locating your nearest fiber shop, I highly recommend writing to *Fiberarts* magazine or one of the large manufacturers listed below. In every issue, *Fiberarts* magazine contains, aside from fabulous articles on artists and exhibits, a long list of small fiber shops. By writing to manufacturers like Stanley Berroco or Belding Lily, you'll find out where their yarns are sold.

Fiberarts Magazine
3717 4th St. N.W.
Albuquerque, NM 87107

Manufacturers

Stanley Berroco Inc.
Mendon Street
Uxbridge, MA 01569

Belding Lily Co. (Lily Mills)
P.O. Box 88
Shelby, NC 28150

Mail-Order Sources

White Sun
708 E. 9th St.
Tucson, AZ 85719

Creative Handweavers
P.O. Box 26480
L.A., CA 90026
Send $2 for samples.

Grandor Industries
4031 Knobhill Drive
Sherman Oaks, CA 91403

Menlo Woolen Mills
851 Hamilton Ave.
Menlo Park, CA 94025
Send $1 for sample cards.

Raye's Eclectic Craft Yarns, Inc.
8157 Commercial St.
La Mesa, CA 92041
Wholesale orders only.

The Yarn Depot
545 Sutter St.
San Francisco, CA 94102
Send $1.50 for samples of stock yarns.

Contessa Yarns
P.O. Box 37
Lebanon, CT 06249
Send 50¢ for samples.

Glass House Fiber Imports
Box 147
Whately, MA 01093
Send $1 for sample cards.

Old Mill Yarn
P.O. Box 8
Eaton Rapids, MI 48827
Send $2 for sample cards.

Wild Weft
415 N. 5th Ave.
Ann Arbor, MI 48104
Send 50¢ for catalog.

Mexiskeins
P.O. Box 1624
Missoula, MT 59801
Send $1.50 for sample cards.

The Sheepish Grin
35 Rockleigh Drive
Trenton, NJ 08628
Send for detailed catalog.

Oregon Worsted
P.O. Box 02098
Portland, OR 97202

Robin & Russ Handweavers
533 N. Adams St.
McMinnville, OR 97128

Index